English Life in
Tudor Times

English Life
in
Tudor Times

Roger Hart

WAYLAND PUBLISHERS · LONDON
G. P. PUTNAMS SONS · NEW YORK

In this series

English Life in Chaucer's Day
English Life in the Seventeenth Century
English Life in the Eighteenth Century
English Life in the Nineteenth Century

Roger Hart

Frontispiece: Guests at Sir Henry Unton's wedding feast

SBN (England): 85340 160 8
SBN (United States): 399–11045–3
Library of Congress Catalog Card Number: 72–84747

Printed in Great Britain by Page Bros (Norwich) Ltd.

Contents

1   The Realm of England

ON 22ND AUGUST, 1485, twenty thousand troops met in bloody battle outside the quiet market town of Bosworth in Leicestershire. At the end of the day, as the cries of the wounded and dying faded away over the open fields, England had a new King for the fourth time within a troubled generation. The victorious Welshman, Henry Tudor, rode south with his armies to London, there to be crowned King Henry VII. His firm rule (1485 to 1509) brought to an end the tangled dynastic Wars of the Roses which for years past had broken the nation's peace. All five Tudor monarchs – Henry VII, Henry VIII, Edward VI, Mary and Elizabeth – were to die in their beds. The House of Tudor was to produce in Henry VII, his son Henry VIII and grand-daughter Elizabeth I, three of the greatest monarchs in English history. In their long reigns England was to lose much of its medieval character, and acquire in its economy, social life, government, religion and other institutions a more modern outlook.

Appearance of England

Despite the intermittent distractions of the Wars of the Roses, life for most of England's two or three million people was dominated by the simple need to survive, and to labour for the bare necessities of food, clothing and shelter. Nine in ten Englishmen lived on the land, for the most part in small village communities isolated even from their near neighbours by a dearth of roads and wheeled transport.

Edward VI (1547–1553)

Below Jousting was a popular sport among Tudor noblemen

It is hard for us, familiar with the ravages of an industrial society, to imagine how little of Tudor England was touched by man at all. Whole tracts of the country were thickly wooded, mainly with deciduous oak forests. As a contemporary rhyme had it,

From Blacon Point to Hillbree
A squirrel may jump from tree to tree.

The great forests included Sherwood, Selwood, the Dean, the Weald, and Arden, with great tracts of uncultivated scrubland in between.

Queen Elizabeth in parliament

These woodlands were still inhabited by many wild animals. Some, such as the wolf, bear, lynx, and elk were by early Tudor times extinct; but wild boar, wildcats and wild cattle were still to be found, as well as the still-surviving red deer. Many of these areas had for hundreds of years been preserved as Royal Forests for the king's hunting.

There were few travellers, except those riding on official business for a great lord or bishop, or perhaps the king. Occasionally, a pedlar or a wandering friar might bring to the villages news of great events in distant parts.

Sixteenth century fashions: a rich merchant and a nobleman *left*,
and yeomen's dress *right*

mercator Londinensis in   Nobilis puellæ ornatus apud Londinenses.   Vulgarium fœminarum in Anglia.   Plebeij adolescentis in Anglia habi
vestitus gentilis.

19

So bad were England's roads, especially in the winter snows and frosts, that it was sometimes impossible to pass from one place to another. Parliament decreed that local people should spend six days each year working to mend the roads in their parish. Unfortunately, however, "The rich do so cancel their portions, and the poor so loiter in their labours, that . . . scarcely two good days' work are well performed." (William Harrison, *Description of England*, 1587).

A further problem was that the parishioners tended to repair not the main roads that led to the next town, but just the little lanes and paths in and around the villages and hamlets. In addition, the stones needed to strengthen the road surfaces were often only sold by local landowners at ridiculous prices.

Harrison had a suggestion to make: "The trees and bushes growing by the streets' sides do not a little keep off the force of the sun in summer for drying up of the lanes. Wherefore, if order were taken that their boughs should continually be kept short, and the bushes not suffered to spread so far into the narrow paths, that inconvenience would also be remedied." Another problem was that roads which once had been fifty feet wide had been steadily encroached upon by neighbouring landowners until they were only twenty or twelve feet wide, making "many an honest man encumbered in his journey."

Duke Frederick of Wurtemberg was appalled at the state of England's roads in 1592. Journeying to Cambridge from London, "We passed through a villanous boggy and wild country, and several times missed our way because the country thereabout is a very little inhabited, and is nearly a waste . . . . There is one spot in particular where the mud is so deep that in my opinion it would scarcely be possible to pass with a coach in winter or in rainy weather."

The isolated villages and hamlets of Tudor England were almost entirely self-supporting and self-generating. There was little movement of population. A visitor from miles away would be treated as warily as a foreigner. The little communities cultivated their own crops, reared sheep for the woollen industry, grew fruit and vegetables and farmed dairy produce. Village craftsmen supplied most local needs – a blacksmith produced iron, farm and domestic implements, shod the horses and acted as a kind of veterinary surgeon; carpenters, thatchers and perhaps a mason put up houses, cottages and barns; a miller ground the corn.

Dominating the village and its affairs would be the local territorial

Above Queen Elizabeth's funeral procession

Opposite Peasants working in their village

11

landlord, who might be a country squire living in a relatively simple style in a timber-framed manor house, or perhaps a great lord whose affairs were conducted by steward and bailiff. The Church, too, exerted a strong moral and practical influence, and the parson was at the centre of such communal social life as the village had, presiding over holy-days at Christmas, Easter and Whitsun, over church-ales, and similar festivities.

Village people rose at dawn and went to bed at dusk. They worked nearly all the hours of daylight except on Sundays. Children worked with their parents, perhaps helping the father in the fields, or assisting the mother with home-spinning or other domestic tasks.

A century before, in 1348, the English countryside had been disastrously depopulated by the murderous bubonic plague from Asia, popularly known as the Black Death. Perhaps a third of England's entire population had perished. This holocaust had quickened the decline of the old feudal system. But by the time of Henry VII, rural life was beset by new problems. The birth rate was beginning once more to outrun the death rate, and many contemporary writers noted a new hunger for land to be brought under cultivation for food.

In many parts of England this living – hard as it was – was made harder still by the demands of the woollen industry for ever more sheep. Tudor England had an enormous sheep population for its size – eight million animals, or about three for every human being. So fast did the sheep overrun precious woodland and arable land that contemporaries began to complain that "sheep do eat up men". The forests were cut down so far that some trees – the oak, birch and hazel – were placed in serious jeopardy.

Small farmers and peasants who depended for their living on cash crops bitterly resented great landowners' preference for sheep farming, and cannot have but welcomed the serious outbreaks of "murrain" (sheep epidemic) which took place in the sixteenth century. Indeed, a rebellion almost amounting to revolution took place in 1549 under Jack Kett, when at the height of the troubles some 20,000 sheep were slaughtered by the people.

These developments produced a whole range of social problems in the countryside. They also produced some new institutions – for example the system by which the rising new class of country clothiers began to have cheap spinning and weaving carried out as a cottage industry by local workers, producing unfinished cloth which would then be exported to the European markets for finishing and re-sale.

This eyewitness account of England's countryside was written by Daniele Barbaro, the Venetian ambassador in London from 1549 to 1550: "Nature has endowed it with great beauty and great bounty, and amongst its chief endowments is that of most fine and excellent wools. 'Tis also rich in metals, having tin and lead in greatest quantity, to such an extent that, in addition to what is used in the island, the worth of two millions in gold is exported to Antwerp as to a centre whence it is distributed to other places."

Barbaro found "animals of all kinds, and such abundant grazing that for a single crown a thousand sheep can be fattened. In some places

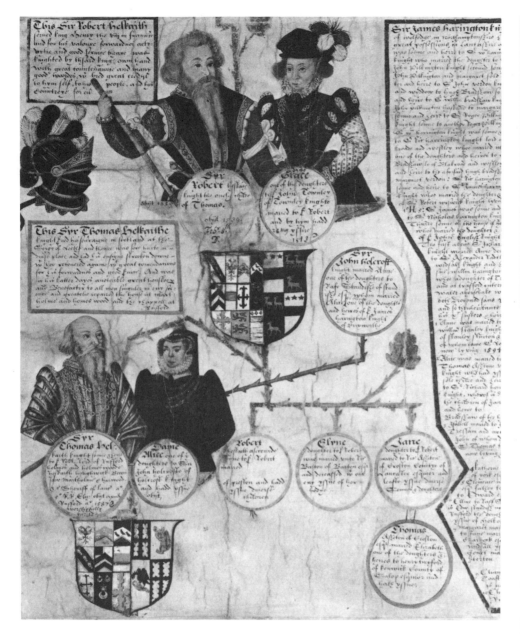

Elaborate Tudor fashions: *above* a nobleman and *below* a noblewoman

Above left Noblemen were proud of their families and sometimes had their family trees beautifully illustrated

grains are plentiful, and they would be much more so if the people did not shirk toil. But they have what they need, and do not seek more . . . .

"Although neither wines nor olives are found there, yet, besides what they procure . . . by their convenient position for sea trade, they can do with less, as they use beer in place of wine, and butter and oil from turnips in place of olive oil. They make salt in several places, and there is no tax on it. They make firewood in abundance, and can procure enough vegetables and saffron, and plenty of fish. Moreover, lodgings are excellent and commodious, a sure sign of the country's wealth."

The Tudor period saw a marked growth of the cities – of which the largest were London, Bristol, York, Norwich, Coventry, Chester and Exeter. Contemporaries marvelled at the size of London, though to a modern visitor it would seem no more than a small town. It grew from

the Strand

Right There were far fewer houses in sixteenth century London than there are today

about 75,000 at the opening of the period to some 200,000 by the death of Queen Elizabeth I in 1603.

But in the earlier Tudor period, the towns were not towns as in the modern sense; they were more like overgrown villages, their lives deeply bound up with that of the surrounding countryside, economically and socially. In their wooden houses they contained only a tenth of England's population, and were typically of 2,000 or 3,000 inhabitants. They had many social problems: the hygiene was extremely primitive – no running water (only wells and pumps), no refuse collection, virtually no knowledge of the infectious nature of diseases and vermin running wild. In addition the accommodation was too densely populated for the good health of the community.

The towns reflected the authoritarian basis of the rest of society. At the top was a governing class of rich merchants, protecting and strengthening their interests through the guilds and courts, and in London through the great livery companies. Lower down the social scale were the lawyers and clerks, small master craftsmen, journeymen and apprentices, independent traders, and domestic servants.

A late Tudor writer remarked that the English were a nation of unbearable snobs. "In London the rich disdain the poor, the courtier the citizen, the citizen the country man. . . . The merchant the retailer, the retailer the craftsman, the better sort of craftsman the baser, the shoemaker the cobbler, the cobbler the carman." Women were just as bad. "One nice dame" will not go to church because she disdains to mix in baser company. She disdains to wear what everyone else wears, or even to hear the same preacher that everyone else hears. "So," adds

Above Queen Elizabeth in parliament

Above left The wife of the Lord Mayor of London at Queen Elizabeth's funeral procession

the writer, "did Jerusalem disdain God's prophets because they came in the likeness of poor men. . . . Their house, for their disdain, was left desolate unto them." (Thomas Nashe, *Christ's Tears Over Jerusalem*, 1593.)

In many ways, the citizens of Tudor England were rather serious and solemn in their outlook on life. Education, religion, family life, work – all were followed with a great degree of gravity. For most people, life was lived under the unchanging shadow of authority: the apprentice working for his master, the schoolboy for his teacher, the tenant for his lord, the priest for his bishop.

One of the finest features of the towns – after the stone churches, and houses of the merchant classes – were their inns. Harrison wrote in 1587 of the "great and sumptuous inns builded in them for the receiving of such travellers and strangers as pass to and fro." He considered the inns better than those elsewhere in Europe. "Every man may use his inn as his own house" and have whatever service he cares to pay for. The rooms were of a high standard, "well furnished with napery [napkins], bedding and tapestry, especially with napery. For beside the linen used at the tables, which is commonly washed daily, is such and so much as belongeth unto the estate and calling of the guest." But though distinctions of class were clearly made, "each comer is sure to lie in clean sheets."

To Harrison, the great value of the inns was that one could regard them as one's own home. "Whether he be horseman or footman, if his chamber be once appointed he may carry the key with him, as of his own house, so long as he lodgeth there." Also, if he lost anything while at the inn, "the host is bound by a general custom to restore the damage,"

Below James I (1603–1625)

15

The Chariot drawne by foure Horses vpon which charret stood the Coffin couered with purple Veluett and vpon that the representation. The Canopy borne by six Knights.

footemen.

so that there was no greater security for an Englishman than in an inn. Their horses were exercized, tended and fed by ostlers employed by the innkeeper, who worked hard in the hope of an extra reward.

Some ostlers were less worthy. They denied the horses their full rations of food and sold the surplus for their own profit. Some were even in league with highwaymen – "slipper merchants which hunt after prey" – who waylaid the hapless traveller after he had left the inn. Few people were robbed by highwaymen, thought Harrison, except where there was collusion with inn servants. A common trick was for the ostler to feel the weight of the traveller's purse, on the pretext of helping him alight from his horse. Inside the inn, the chamberlain (room servant) would move the visitor's wallet from one part of the room to another, pretending to tidy the room, but really to feel the weight of the coins, and to decide whether he would be worth robbing on the highway after he left the inn. At the bar, too, "the tapster . . . doth mark his [the visitor's] behaviour, and what plenty of money he draweth when he payeth the shot [drink]."

In all the country's inns, Harrison found plenty of ale, beer and wine. Some inns were so large that they could hold two or three hundred people, together with their horses, and feed both with a speed and efficiency that to those unacquainted with it seemed incredible. London contained both the best and the worst of England's inns, though most were better than those on the continent. "It is a world to see how each owner of them contendeth with other for goodness of entertainment of their guests, as about fineness and change of linen, furniture of bedding, beauty of rooms, service at the table, costliness of plate, strength of drink, variety of wines, or well using of horses." Every inn had its inn sign and, if Harrison is to be believed, some innkeepers spent thirty or forty pounds – a large sum in the Tudor period – on commissioning them – "a mere vanity in my opinion." But good signs were good for business.

A Tudor knight

"Lovers of shew"

Let us end this preview of Tudor England with a German opinion of the English people. In his *Travels in England* (1598), Otto Hentzner wrote: "The English are serious like the Germans, lovers of shew, liking to be followed wherever they go by whole troops of servants, who wear their masters' arms in silver, fastened to their left arms, a ridicule they deservedly lay under. They excel in dancing and music, for they are active and lively, though of a thicker make than the French. They cut their hair close on the middle of the head, letting it grow on either side; they are good sailors – and better pirates – cunning, treacherous, and thievish. Above three hundred are said to be hanged annually at London. Beheading with them is less infamous than hanging; they give the wall as the place of honour; hawking is the general sport of the gentry.

"They are more polite in eating than the French, devouring less bread, but more meat, which they roast in perfection; they put a great deal of sugar in their drink; their beds are covered with tapestry, even those of farmers; they are often molested with the scurvy, said to have

A yeoman of the guard

first crept into England with the Norman conquest. Their houses are commonly of two storeys, except in London, where they are of three and four, though but seldom of four; they are built of wood, those of the richer sort with bricks; their roofs are low, and, where the owner has money, covered with lead.

"They are powerful in the field, successful against their enemies, impatient of anything like slavery; vastly fond of great noises that fill the ear, such as the firing of cannon, drums, and the ringing of bells, so that it is common for a number of them, that have got a glass in their heads, to go up into some belfry and ring the bells for hours together for the sake of the exercise. If they see a foreigner very well made, or particularly handsome, they will say, 'It is a pity he is not an Englishman'!"

2 *Rural Life*

TUDOR ENGLAND was predominantly an agricultural land. In villages and manors from the West Country to the lawless North, faraway from the seat of government in London, the gentry and independent yeomen farmed their land. The gentry and nobility let part of their land to small tenants on a variety of tenures, and farmed part – their "demesne" – themselves. The hard seasonal work of ploughing, harrowing, sowing, reaping and harvesting was mainly done by villeins and peasants whose life in some respects had barely changed since the middle ages. On the squire's land, peasants sometimes in a state of effective bondage laboured under the eye of the steward and bailiff, being paid partly in goods and partly in coin. Work was hard, beginning at dawn and ending at dusk.

A yeoman farmer measuring his land

Rents

"The improvement of the ground," remarked Francis Bacon, "is the most natural obtaining of riches . . . . But it is slow. And yet where men of great wealth do stoop to husbandry, it multiplieth riches exceedingly." The Tudor period was a time of great change and social unrest in the countryside. The sixteenth century was hit by acute inflation, in which men of all classes suffered – tenant farmers whose rents were doubled and quadrupled, and landowners whose tenants were on long leases where often the rents could not be raised to keep pace with the cost of living. As Edward VI observed in 1551, the estates of gentlemen and nobles "has alone not increased the gain of living . . . . Their house-keeping is dearer, their liveries dearer, their wages greater."

Enclosures

For hundreds of years landlords had "enclosed" their land with permanent hedges to achieve better results from the land. But in Tudor times this movement was intensified. Wasteland and forest were cleared and enclosed for arable farming, and for pasturing of sheep. Often these enclosures were carried out to the satisfaction of local people, but sometimes a squire or nobleman anxious to increase and protect his agriculture would not scruple to get rid of smaller or weaker tenants who stood in his way. Many people who were dispossessed in this way complained bitterly about the enclosures of land for sheep pasture: "Where forty persons had their livings, now one man and his shepherd hath all." As this versifier put it:

> Sheepe have eate up our medows and our downes,
> Our corne, our wood, whole villages and townes.
> Yea, they have eate up many wealthy men,
> Besides widowes and Orphane childeren:
> Besides our statutes and our iron lawes
> Which they have swallowed down into their maws.
> Till now I thought the proverbe did but jest,
> Which said a blacke sheepe was a biting beast.

Yet many landlords had no choice but to use every method to try and improve their revenues from the land. The massive price rise which took place in the Tudor period forced them to rethink and replan their land use, often to sheep pasture, or be ruined by household expenses. To them, as to Thomas Tusser, the benefits of enclosure were clear:

> More plenty of mutton and beef
> Corn, butter and cheese of the best,
> More wealth anywhere (to be brief)
> More people, more handsome and prest,
> Where find ye (go search any coast)
> Than there, where enclosures are most?

As A. H. Dodd has written, "The classes most liable to suffer from all this [i.e. enclosure] were naturally those with the most precarious tenures: copyholders for life, tenants at will, cottagers accustomed to some 'refreshing' on the commons . . . . The blame was generally laid at the door of successful merchants stepping out of their class to buy up manors and lordships and treating them as business investments as well as avenues to gentility."

The following is an interesting example of the outcry that took place early in the reign of Henry VIII, in 1514, at enclosures near London: "Before this time the towns about London, as Islington, Hoxton,

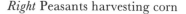

Right Peasants harvesting corn

Above Village women doing their laundry in a stream

Below Wool was an important product of Tudor England and shepherds had large flocks of sheep to mind

Shepherds minding sheep

Shoreditch and other, had so enclosed the common fields with hedges and ditches, that neither the young men of the City might shoot, nor the ancient persons might walk for their pleasure in the fields, except either the bows and arrows were broken or taken away, or the honest and substantial persons arrested or indicted, saying that no Londoner should go out of the City but in the highways.

"This saying sore grieved the Londoners, and suddenly this year a great number of the City assembled themselves in a morning, and a turner in a fool's coat came crying through the City – "Shovels and spades!" – and so many people followed that it was a wonder, and within a short space all the hedges about the towns were cast down, and the ditches filled, and everything made plain [level], the workmen were so diligent.

"The King's Council, hearing of this assembly, came to the Greyfriars, and sent for the Mayor and the Council of the City to know the cause, which declared to them the nuisance done to the Citizens, and their commodities and liberties taken from them, though they would not that the commonalty and young persons, which were dampnified [depressed] by the nuisance, would pluck up and remedy the same.

"And when the King's Council had heard the answer, they dissimuled the matter, and commanded the Mayor to see that no other thing were attempted, and to call home the Citizens, which, when they had done their enterprise, came home before the King's Council and the Mayor departed, without any harm more doing, and so after the fields were never hedged."

Another writer's "father was a yeoman, and had no lands of his own, only he had a farm of £3 or £4 per year at the uttermost, and here upon he tilled so much as kept half a dozen men. He had walk for a hundred sheep, and my mother milked 30 kine [cattle]. . . . He kept me to school. . . . He married my sisters with £5 or 20 nobles* apiece. . . . He kept hospitality for his poor neighbours. And some alms he gave to the poor, and all this did he of the said farm." But rents were rising with enclosures, and "he that now has it, pays £16 by year and more, and is not able to do anything . . . for himself, nor for his children, or

Towns people were often very fashionable and made fun of country fashions

* A measure of money now obsolete.

A sixteenth century kitchen

give a cup of drink to the poor." The encloser was often condemned as a "cormorant", or "greedy gull" or "cruel kestrel":

> *Houses by three, and seven, and ten he raseth*
> *To make the common glebe his private land:*
> *Our country cities cruel he defaceth;*
> *The grass grows green* [i.e. for sheep] *where Troy did stand.*

Above Cleaning mineral ores

Although many people did suffer with enclosures, a large part of this intensified enclosure movement was concerned with "colonization" – bringing into agricultural use farm and wasteland which was previously wild country, still inhabited by many species of wild animal that were soon to disappear from the English countryside. In many ways, the farming methods in use were those of the medieval period – the plough-team, although horses were coming to be preferred to oxen to draw them, and the ploughs were fitted more generously with iron; rye was still the predominant cereal crop. But there were changes. Some counties were gaining a reputation for specializing in certain types of produce – Kent for its hops and fruit orchards, East Anglia for its barley, Cheshire and Suffolk for their cheeses. A notable feature of the Tudor period, too, was the growing output of books on "good husbandry".

Below A coppersmith

Although part of the rural middle class suffered from enclosures, in the main it prospered. Sixteenth century prose and verse is full of praise for the "yeoman" class and for its solid virtues. These were men who farmed their own land and consumed their own produce. They often lived plainly, but extremely well, and did not have the expenses of the superior gentry class, with its manor houses and servants to support. Many of the yeoman had secure tenures, and so to a large degree could prosper from efficient farming, without being hit too hard by the price rise of the century.

A description of yeomen was given by William Harrison. "For the most part the yeomen are farmers to gentlemen. And with grazing, frequenting of markets, and keeping of servants (not idle servants as gentlemen do, but such as get their own and part of their masters'

Shepherds holding their crooks

A country woman wearing a muffler to keep the dust out of her mouth

living) so come to great wealth, insomuch that many of them are able, and do, buy the lands of unthrifty gentlemen, and often setting their sons to the schools and to the Universities and to the Inns of Court; or otherwise leaving them sufficient lands whereupon they may live without labour, do make them by those means to become gentlemen."

This yeoman class played an important part in national defence by serving in the county militias, which were relied upon by the government in the absence of a regular standing army. As Harrison wrote, "There is almost no village so poor in England, be it never so small, that it hath not sufficient furniture in a readiness to set forth three or four soldiers, as one archer, one gunner, one pike, and a billman at the least. The said armour and munition is kept in one several place appointed by consent of the whole parish, where it is always ready to be had and worn within an hour warning." From 1557 the man in charge of the militia was the Lord Lieutenant of the County, appointed by the Queen, instead of the Sheriff as before.

It was usually official policy to encourage warlike sports. One of these, archery, was specially encouraged by Henry VIII in an Act of 1541 "for the maintenance of artillery and the debarring of unlawful games." The first treatise on English archery was published in 1545 by Roger Ascham, *Toxophilus*. But the bow, on which English troops had for so long relied, slowly but surely yielded place to fire arms. Bows and arrows were finally discarded as real weapons in England in 1595, and even fell into disuse in the hunting field. Fencing, too, was encouraged by Henry VIII, and during the sixteenth century many Italian fencing schools were founded in England, and every gentleman learned how to defend himself with rapier and dagger.

Thomas Platter recorded a general level of improvement in English farming by the end of the century. In his *Travels in England* (1599) he found a splendid profusion of field crops – corn, rye, barley, oats, beans, hops, garden produce, apples, pears, purple plums, and cherries. Deer abounded, "both in the woods and in enclosed parks; likewise red deer, stags and other game, small in size and quantity however." He praised England's great and thriving wool industry: "Sheep are abundant, and since there are no wolves in England they are easier to keep. The wool is extremely good and the cloth is rated very high."

The Parish

The local unit of rural life, even more than the manor or the family, was the parish and its centre the parish church. The parish priest, usually assisted by a parish clerk and perhaps a beadle and sexton, was an important figure in local affairs. He was probably the only man with any education in the village. He often dined each week with the local gentry, and supplemented his income by acting as the squire's chaplain.

The parish was also an economic force to some extent; Queen Mary I made each parish elect its own surveyor of highways, to serve unpaid for a year at a time. It was his job to raise parish funds for filling in ruts and pot-holes. But in many areas the job was neglected, and the scheme,

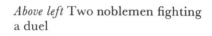

Most men in Tudor times were
skilled archers

Above left Two noblemen fighting
a duel

Duelling was a common means of
settling disputes among noblemen

A gardener pruning a fruit tree

which had been designed as a nationwide effort to improve, or at least maintain, England's roads, was only partly successful.

In other ways, the Tudor period was important in the evolution of the parish; in the time of Henry VIII, the parson had also been made the registrar of births, marriages and deaths, an important landmark for social historians and genealogists. Overseers had to be appointed to deal with poverty and vagabondage; and the petty constable had to assist the churchwardens in making sure that all the villagers went to church on Sundays.

The problem of Sunday observance was a vexing one. As Archbishop Cranmer told his clergy in 1547, "In our time, God is more offended than pleased, more dishonoured than honoured upon the holy day, because of idleness, pride, drunkenness, quarrelling and brawling, which are most used in such days, people nevertheless persuading themselves sufficiently to honour God that day if they hear mass and service, though they understand nothing to their edifying." And in Queen Elizabeth's time, too, "Fairs and markets in most towns are usually kept upon the Sabbath . . . wakes, ales, greenes, May-games, rush-bearings, bear-baites, dove-ales, bonfires, all manner unlawful gaming, piping and dancing and suchlike, are in all places freely exercized upon the Sabbath . . . so that it were hard for the preacher to find a competent congregation in any church to preach unto" (1590).

The greatest religious change in the Tudor period was, of course, the Reformation of the Church by Henry VIII, when the tie with the Papacy in Rome was broken, and the orders of monks and friars dissolved, their monasteries and lands sold off mainly to the nobility. But the Reformation was more than simply the result of a desperate King's attempt to divorce and remarry in order to beget a legitimate male heir to the throne. There were changes in the form of the prayer-book, and of religious services and the furnishing of churches, which affected the life of every village churchgoer. As William Harrison noted in 1587, "Bells, and times of morning and evening prayer, remain as in times past, saving that all images, shrines, tabernacles, roodlofts and monuments of idolatry are removed, taken down and defaced." Also, the Bible had now been translated into English.

The people of rural England were as superstitious as they were religious. Belief in witchcraft goes back to the very earliest times, but the Tudor period saw a resurgence of interest in the subject, prompted very largely by the savage persecutions which were taking place in Germany, France and elsewhere in Europe at the time. The poet Edmund Spenser (1552–1599) described the popular idea of a witch:

> *There in a gloomy hollow glen, she found*
> *A little cottage built of sticks and weeds,*
> *In homely wise, and walled with sods around,*
> *In which a witch did dwell in loathly weeds*
> *And wilfull want, all careless of her needs;*
> *So choosing solitary to abide*
> *Far from all neighbours, that her devilish deeds*
> *And hellish art from people she might hide,*
> *And hurt far off, unknown, whomever she envied.*

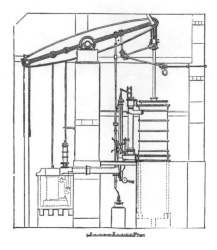

A sixteenth-century steam pumping machine

Pedlars were a common sight at fairs and festivals

Right Vine growing and wine making were much more common in Tudor times than now

The first law against witchcraft passed in England was enacted by Henry VIII in 1542. If anyone should "use, devise, practise or exercize . . . any invocations or conjurations of spirits, witchcrafts, enchantments or sorceries, to find money or treasure, or to waste, consume or destroy any person . . . or dig up or pull down any cross . . . [They will suffer] such pains of death, loss and forfeitures of their lands, tenants, goods and chattels, as in case of felony [and] lose privilege of the clergy and sanctuary." A similar, but wider act, was passed early in the reign of Elizabeth I, in 1563. But most of the action against witches was launched not by the government in pursuance of these and other measures, but by local villagers and townspeople filled with superstition; and the normal punishments were the ducking stool and the stocks. The first major English witchcraft trial, however, took place at Chelmsford three years after the passing of Elizabeth's statute. This seemed to spark off a regular wave of witchcraft in the county of Essex, and further trials and hangings took place there a few years later. The basis on which the sentences were brought in were highly questionable; hearsay evidence was eagerly accepted, and some of the victims were hanged on their own confessions, without any corroboration. These events prompted some people to question the whole subject, and Reginald Scot published his famous and sceptical *The Discoverie of Witchcraft* in 1584. But the stage was being set for the persecution of "witches" which was to reach its peak under the Stuarts in the seventeenth century, when the self-appointed "witchfinder-general" Matthew Hopkins came to fame, or infamy.

Agnes Sampson being punished by King James

Left Agnes Sampson, a witch said to have raised a storm against King James's ship in 1591

Bottom left Countrywomen returning from market

A nobleman giving alms to a beggar

Water carriers were useful people because there was no running water

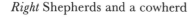

The country poor

Every village and county had its beggars and vagabonds. In 1495, Henry VII passed an Act against vagabondage, ordering parish officials to give all vagabonds, idle persons and beggars, a spell in the stocks, and then eject them from the town. Infirm beggars should be ejected, too, and sent back to their own parish to beg for alms there.

An Act passed by Henry VIII in 1531 drew a new distinction between those beggars who were genuinely infirm, and "sturdy beggars" who had no good reason for idleness. The infirm beggars were henceforth to obtain a licence from the local justices of the peace permitting them to beg. The "sturdy beggars" on the other hand, especially those found straying from their home locality, were treated with great severity, being condemned to a whipping at the cart-tail, and then sent packing with a certificate of their punishment and dire warnings about coming back. Another Act passed five years later added the cutting off of one ear to the penalties of vagabonds who refused work for no good reason. On the other hand, local villagers were exhorted to be generous in almsgiving to the really needy; vagrants tramping back to their own villages became entitled to a free meal from the local constable at each stage of ten miles on the way home. For those who did find work, life was hard. A statute of 1495 laid down that workmen should start work in the months from March to September by five in the morning, and finish between seven and eight o'clock at night, with half an hour for breakfast, and an hour for dinner.

But much of this legislation was ineffective. The problem was too general, and in any case there was no-one to enforce the law. Enforcement was left entirely in the hands of local people, notably the justices of the peace, who were sometimes intimidated by beggars in their district, who might burn down barns or commit other damage to property unless they were left in peace.

In the middle of the Tudor period the problem grew even worse. The pressure of the enclosure movement was making many people destitute, for example tenants-at-will and the sons of copyholders whose land had been taken over by an enclosing landlord trying to cope with economic problems of his own. It has been estimated that for each plough lost in favour of sheep farming, six people lost their traditional jobs. One parson commented in 1550, "If the poor oppressed complain

Right Shepherds and a cowherd

to the justices of the peace or suchlike in the county where he dwelleth that hath the injury done unto him, little redress, as I hear, can be had."

Apart from the problems arising from enclosures there were many social problems arising from the dissolution of the monasteries by Henry VIII, and the sale of their lands which ensued. The monks and abbots had not been known as good landlords. As a versifier put it:

> *How have the abbeys their payment?*
> *A new way they do invent*
> *Letting a dozen farms under one,*
> *Which one or two rich franklins*
> *Occupying a dozen men's livings*
> *Take all in their own hands alone.*

> *

> *Where a farm for twenty pounds was set,*
> *Under thirty they would not let.*

But as the monastic lands were taken by Henry VIII, partly for himself, and partly for sale to courtiers to raise funds for his depleted exchequer, the insecurity of the tenants was often greater still. Many of the courtiers took advantage of the changes to press on with enclosures. In addition, although most of the monks and friars could make a living elsewhere, in schools for example, their armies of servants and dependants could not. These "hangers-on" of the once-rich monasteries enjoyed little public sympathy. They were denounced as "idle abbey-lubbers, apt to do nothing but only eat and drink." Many of them now became destitute, and the need to tackle the problem of poverty grew more pressing. Many people felt that the dissolution of the monasteries might have been an excellent opportunity to make endowments for the benefit of the poor. But:

> *The lands and jewels that hereby were had*
> *Would have found goodly preachers which might well have led*
> *The people aright that now go astray,*
> *And have fed the poor that famish every day.*

London, as in other spheres, took the lead in dealing with destitution. St. Bartholomew's Hospital had been endowed to provide 100 beds, a physician and three surgeons to care for the sick poor. Bethlehem Hospital – "Bedlam" for short – was in use for the sick in mind, though the predominance of music, darkened rooms, poor diet and the whip testified to the Tudors' lack of understanding of the inmates, who already were being visited as a "peepshow" by the general public. Christ's Hospital cared for destitute children, and set standards of education that were to make it a great public school. St. Thomas's Hospital, south of the River Thames in Southwark, was a place of refuge for those too infirm to work, while Edward VI appointed Bridewell as a "house of correction" for idle vagabonds. Other cities followed this enterprising lead of the metropolis, and soon hospitals and schools were growing in Lincoln, Norwich, Cambridge, Ipswich and elsewhere.

The sons of noble families were usually trained as page boys

But the problem of the sick and destitute was a national one. The measures taken by the earlier Tudors had proved largely ineffective. In Queen Elizabeth's reign a series of measures of poor relief were enacted which began to make a positive contribution to the problem.

Country pleasures

Life might have been intolerable for country folk but for wild outbreaks of riotous merriment several times a year. May Day, heralding the arrival of spring, was one such occasion, celebrated with festivities that were nakedly pagan. The Puritan, Philip Stubbes, wrote that on the eve of May Day the people of every parish, town and village would go "some to the woods and groves, some to the hills and mountains" where they would spend the night in "pleasant pastimes", returning in the morning with birch boughs and branches of trees "to deck their assemblies withal." In a tone of extreme disapproval he remarked, "And no wonder, for there is a great lord present among them . . . namely Satan, Prince of Hell." The villagers' main trophy from the hillsides was the maypole, which they would carry home with great veneration with the aid of twenty or forty yoke of oxen, each animal having its horns decked with nosegays. The maypole – "this stinking idol" – was covered all over with flowers and herbs and tied with strings and ribbons, and followed in procession to the village green by all the local people. "And thus being reared up with handkerchiefs and flags streaming on top, they straw the ground about, bind green boughs around it, set up summer halls, bowers and arbours hard by it. And then they fall to banquet and feast, to leap and dance about it, as the heathen people did at the dedication of their idols." (*Anatomy of Abuses*, 1583).

All over the country, villagers celebrated their own local occasions. The origins of some of these are lost in antiquity. Riding home from

Acrobats were a popular entertainment at fairs

Above left A Tudor knot garden

Above Boys fishing from a river

London, Bishop Hugh Latimer once entered a village on a Sunday to find the church doors locked. At last, someone came to him and said, "Sir, this is a busy day with us, we cannot hear you, it is Robin Hood's day. The parish are gone abroad to gather for Robin Hood." Latimer wrote afterwards, "It is no laughing matter my friends, it is a weeping matter . . . to prefer Robin Hood before the ministration of God's word."

One of the best known festivities which took place each year in England for many years, was the crowning of the Lord of Misrule – sometimes known as the Feast of Fools. Stubbes wrote, "First, all the wildheads of the parish . . . choose them a Grand Captain of all mischief whom they ennoble with the title of Lord of Misrule, and him they crown with great solemnity and adopt for their king. This king anointed chooses twenty, forty, three score or an hundred lusty guts, like to himself, to wait upon his lordly majesty and to guard his noble person." These "lusty guts" then decked themselves out in liveries, usually in green, yellow, brown, or other colours of Nature, and put on "scarfs, ribbons, and laces, hanged all over with gold rings, precious stones and other jewels. This done, they tie about their legs twenty or forty bells, with rich handkerchiefs in their hands."

Below Transporting fish

Thus attired, the Lord of Misrule and his followers went on a rampage through their town or village, sometimes with hobby-horses, or dragon mascots, "their pipers piping, their drummers drumming, their stumps dancing, their bells jingling, their handkerchiefs swinging about their heads like madmen, their hobby-horses and other monsters skirmishing amongst the throng." They stormed into the parish church, regardless of the minister, "like devils incarnate". And the simple village folk would watch in wonderment at these antics, standing up on the pews to watch the uproar. Finally, after more dancing, much drunkenness and debauch, "these terrestrial furies" came to the end of their sabbath, and the end of the one-day reign of the Lord of Misrule.

A nobleman training a falcon

A lady wearing a special skirt to protect her clothes from dirt while travelling

A water carrier

Many people, mainly those of a Puritan outlook, sought to put a stop to such rowdy rural pleasures. Philip Stubbes wrote: "Every country, city, town, village and other place hath abundance of ale-houses, taverns and inns, which are so fraught with malt-worms, night and day, that you would wonder to see them. You shall have them there sitting at the wine and good-ale all the day long, yea, all the night too, per-adventure a whole week together, so long as any money is left, swilling, gulling and carousing from one to another, till never a one can speak a ready word. Then, when with the spirit of the buttery they are thus possessed, a world it is to consider their gestures and demeanours . . . . How they stut and stammer, stagger and reel to and fro like madmen . . . and, which is most horrible, some fall to swearing, cursing and banning, interlacing their speeches with curious terms of blasphemy. . . ." Nor did Stubbes have much time for the cruel sport of bearbaiting: "The baiting of a bear, besides that it is a filthy, stinking, and loathsome game, is it not a dangerous and a perilous exercise, wherein a man is in danger of his life every minute of an hour? . . . What Christian heart can take pleasure to see one poor beast to rent, tear, and kill another, and all for his foolish pleasure?"

An equally cruel and popular country sport, with ancient origins, was cock-fighting. Thomas Platter wrote in 1599: "I saw the place which is built like a theatre. In the centre on the floor stands a circular table covered with straw and with ledges round it, where the cocks are teased and incited to fly at one another, while those with wagers as to which cock will win, sit closest around the circular disk, but the specta-tors who are merely present on their entrance penny sit around higher up, watching with eager pleasure the fierce and angry fight between the cocks, as these wound each other to death with spurs and beaks. And the party whose cock surrenders or dies loses the wager."

Football is often thought to be a noisy and violent game today, but if Philip Stubbes is right it bears no comparison with the bloody fights that took place in Elizabethan England. It was "a bloody and murdering practice. . . . Sometimes their necks are broken, sometimes their backs, sometimes their legs, sometimes their arms, sometimes one part thrust out of joint. . . . Sometimes their noses gush out with blood, sometimes their eyes start out." There were no rules: anyone holding the ball had to run for his life, else they will "hit him under the short ribs with their gripped fists, and with their knees to catch him upon the hip. . . ." All in all, said Stubbes, football was the father of "envy, malice, rancour, choler, hatred, displeasure, enmity, and what not else."

Gentle pursuits

In the time of the Tudors the English countryside remained heavily wooded. Many of the great forests which existed then are but names on a map today. These great forests provided a rich hunting ground for kings, queens and the great men of the realm, and a rich poaching ground for local people hunting for a tasty addition to the cooking pot.

Every manor house of substance had its own deer park, an attraction to every local poacher. Deer were the greatest prizes, although hare, bustards and foxes were also hunted, on foot or on horseback. The Tudors were not particular how they caught their prey. Sometimes the deer were chased into specially prepared ambushes, and shot with the cross-bow. "Under this thick-grown brake we'll shroud ourselves," says the keeper in Shakespeare's *Henry VI.* Queen Elizabeth was a keen hunter herself, and once had to put off seeing the French ambassador and take to her bed for several days to recover from her exhaustion.

In his *Country Contentments* (1611) Gervase Markham described hunting as "a curious search or conquest of one beast over another . . . accomplished by the diversities and distinctions of smells only. . . ." The quarry were many and varied – stag, buck, roe, hare, fox, badger, otter, boar, goat and other creatures. In Elizabethan England many books were written about hunting, "the noble art of venerie." For example, in 1576 George Turberville had some hints on preparing for the chase. "Immediately after supper the huntsman should go to his master's chambers – and if he serve a king let him go to the Master of Game's chamber – to know his pleasure in what quarter he determineth to hunt the day following." That done, he should go to bed, and in the morning take a draught of wine, and give his hounds a little to eat. "And let him not forget to fill his bottle with good wine." Then, he should "take a little vinegar in the palm of his hand, and put it in the nostrils of the hound, for to make him snuff, to the end his scent may be the perfecter."

This was a superstitious age, and the wary hunstmen kept an eye open for omens good and bad before the hunt began. "If he chance by the way to find any hare, partridge or any other beast or bird that is fearful, living upon seeds or pasturage, it is an evil sign or presage that he shall have but evil pastime that day. But if he find any beast or ravine, living upon prey, as wolf, fox, raven and suchlike, that is a token of good luck."

Gervase Markham believed that a good pack of hunting hounds should be chosen partly for the sound of its barking. "You must compound it of some large dogs that have deep solemn mouths [to] bear the bass in consort, then a double number of roaring and loud ringing mouths which must bear the counter-tenor, then some hollow plain sweet mouths which must bear the mean or middle part." All this would give "much sweetness to the solemnness and graveness of the cry, and the music thereof will be much more delightful to the ears of every beholder."

After hunting, falconry was the most popular sport of the country gentry. "An if a man have not skill in the hawking and hunting language I'll not give a rush for him." Much time was devoted to the skilled art of training the hawk to bring down the heron, bittern, wild duck, partridges, pheasants and woodcock which were its main prey. Dogs were used in falconry, as in hunting, establishing the reputation of the English as a nation of dog-lovers, and especially of greyhounds. The fowler preferred to catch his birds with a variety of mechanical instruments – the bird-bolt, springs, lime, and even fire-arms, "fowling pieces" such as the caliver.

A countrywoman riding to market

Falconing was a popular sport among the aristocracy

3 Town Life

THE TOWNS of Tudor England remained largely medieval in character. Often they were little more than overgrown villages, conveniently sited for road or river transport, or perhaps grown up around a large cathedral or monastic foundation. The lives of the townsfolk were inextricably bound up with the surrounding farmlands and woodlands. In the narrow streets, sometimes cobbled, more often muddy tracks, craftsmen and tradesmen and their families carried on their precarious existence under the ever-present threats of plague and death and other sudden disasters for which the world then had no insurance. As they had done for centuries past, they worked as weavers and sellers of cloth, tailors and leathermakers, or vendors of market and dairy produce brought in from the surrounding manors, or making the metal and wooden implements used in building, agriculture and other industries.

The largest towns in England after London, the capital, were Norwich, the centre of the textile industry; Bristol, the nation's second port, with customs revenues only a twentieth of those of London; and York, the effective capital of the lawless north, removed by several days hard riding from the more peaceful and settled south. But none of these had more than about 10,000 to 20,000 inhabitants. Accurate figures are impossible to find, since the registration of births, marriages and deaths was only made compulsory in the middle of the sixteenth century by Queen Mary I.

Every town's affairs were dominated in large measure by a local territorial magnate. As Sir Walter Raleigh recorded, "Even our cities and corporations here in England – such as need the protection of great men – complain otherwise of their patrons' overmuch overbearance, either in searching into their private estates, or behaving themselves master-like in point of government." Many boroughs sought to be represented in Parliament not by their own burgesses, but by powerful members of the nobility or gentry who, in return for local commercial advantages or commercial revenues, for example from markets, would press local interests at Westminster and the Court.

Within most towns, commercial life was coming to be dominated by small oligarchies of rich merchants, many of whom had complete control over local industry. These men enforced apprenticeships, which incidentally ensured them a constant supply of cheap labour; they regulated markets and fairs, with their standards of quality and prices;

Opposite above Newcastle: towns were much smaller than they are today.
Below A Tudor street with timbered buildings

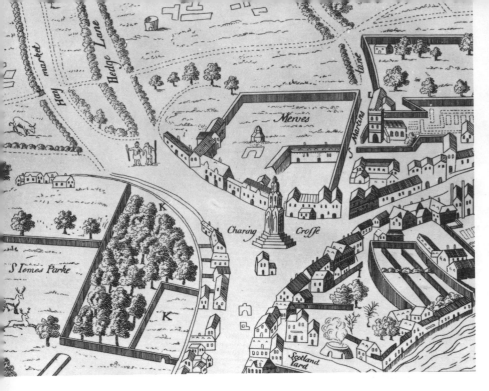

Above: left Tudor London; *right* Westminster Palace in the sixteenth century

Dyeing cloth

and they settled disputes between one commercial group and another. These local dignitaries also kept a close watch on morals, drunkenness and brawling. They organized bellmen and watchmen to look after town security after nightfall:

Twelve o'clock, look well to your locks,
Your fire and your light, and so good night.

As Sir Walter Raleigh indicated, the prosperous classes in the towns were almost as much caught up in a feudal-style relationship as the peasants, villeins and tenant farmers in the countryside. The seven-year apprentice was bound to his master by rules of obedience reinforced by penalties for misconduct; the master was ruled by his craft guild.

Foreigners did not think much of the way the English treated their children, often sending the younger sons to be apprenticed to learn a trade. One Italian wrote, "The want of affection in the English is strongly manifested towards their children; for after having kept them at home till they arrive at the age of seven or nine years at the utmost, they put them out, both males and females, to hard service in the houses of other people, binding them generally for another seven or nine years.

"And these are called apprentices, and during that time they perform all the most menial offices; and few are born who are exempted from this fate, for every one, however rich he may be, sends away his children into the houses of others, whilst he, in return, receives those of strangers into his own. And on inquiring their reason for this severity, they answered that they did it in order that their children might learn better manners. But I, for my part, believe that they do it because they like to enjoy all their comforts themselves, and that they are better served by strangers than they would be by their own children."

Harrison noted that the wage-earning class, though free from the taint of servile position, "have neither voice nor authority in the Commonwealth. Yet they are not altogether neglected, for in cities and corporate towns, for default of yeomen, they are fain to make up their inquest of such meaner people."

London

London was one of the greatest cities in sixteenth century Europe. It was also far and away the largest city in England. Its population was perhaps 75,000 in Henry VII's time, and this trebled by the time of Queen Elizabeth's death in 1603. It attracted the praise and admiration of many visitors, provincial and foreign. A Scottish poet, probably William Dunbar, wrote:

> *Strong be thy walls that about thee stand;*
> *Wise be thy people that within thee dwell;*
> *Fresh be thy river, with his lusty strand;*
> *Blithe be thy churches; well sounding be thy bells;*
> *Rich be thy merchants that in substance excels;*
> *Fair be thy wives, right lovesome, white and small;*
> *Clear be thy virgins, lusty under kells;*
> *London, thou are the flower of Cities all.*

Horses were the commonest form of travel, so blacksmiths were much in demand

Other visitors, especially those from Europe, marvelled at the craftsmanship of London tradesmen. An Italian wrote about 1500, "It abounds with every article of luxury, but the most remarkable thing in London is the wonderful quantity of wrought silver. In one single street, named the Strand, leading to St. Paul's, there are fifty-two goldsmiths' shops, so rich and full of silver vessels. And those vessels are all either salt-cellars or drinking-cups, or basins to hold water for the hands, for they eat off that fine tin, which is little inferior to silver [i.e. pewter]."

Indeed, London enjoyed many natural advantages – it had a good port quite near the prosperous Netherlands; it had its own flourishing local industries, and rich farmland and orchards nearby in Kent and Essex; and it had the broad channel of the River Thames. It also formed the centre of England's road system, such as it was. The seat of Parliament was at Westminster; the monarchy ruled from the Palace of St. James, and there were the courts of justice at Westminster, too. London was also the hub of commercial life. The clothiers had their great Blackwell Hall in Basinghall Street, the lead manufacturers Leadenhall, the merchants of the Hanse the Steelyard. Other groups had their halls, too, for example the Merchant Taylors, Goldsmiths, Skinners and Haberdashers. These fine buildings were not only the places where merchants gathered together to conduct their business, they were also splendid monuments, rivalling churches and cathedrals, often built in stone, testifying to the prosperity and enterprise of their members.

Above Goldsmiths at work

Below A tailor with his two apprentices

The River Thames had many wharves and steps along its banks where goods could be loaded and unloaded. One of the most famous riverside markets was the fish market at Billingsgate. The Thames was a focal point for recreation. In his *Travels in England* (1599) Thomas Platter found that people would "cross the water, or travel up and down the town . . . by attractive pleasure craft, for a number of tiny streets lead to the Thames from both ends of the town. The boatmen wait there in great crowds, each one eager to be first to catch one, for all are free to choose the ship they find most attractive and pleasing." The wherries were charmingly upholstered, with embroidered cushions laid across

A bookbinder

Shipping on the River Thames

Washing gold

The custom house in Queen Elizabeth's reign

A tailor's shop

Right Eastcheap, one of London's market thoroughfares

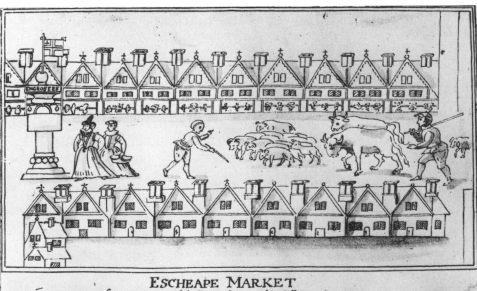

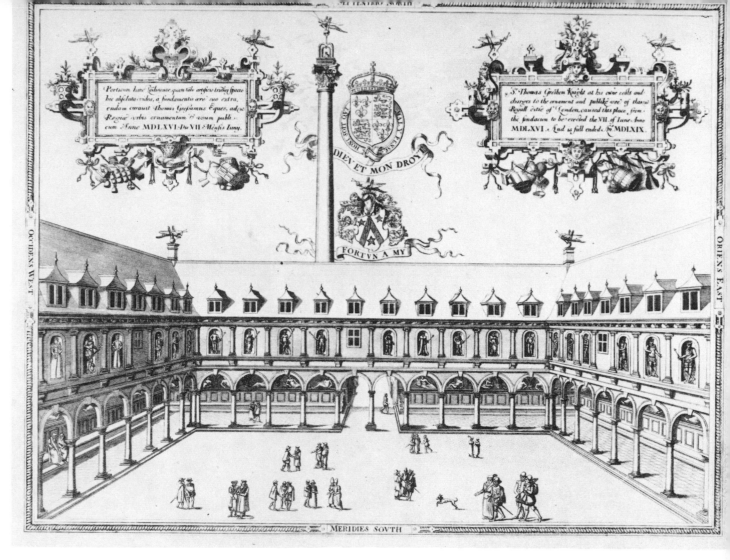

The Royal Exchange where merchants bought and sold goods

the seats. They were thought very comfortable to travel in. "Many of them are covered in, particularly in rainy weather or fierce sunshine."

Dominating the London skyline as dramatically as the skyscrapers of Manhattan, New York, do today, were the scores of church spires. The tallest spire of all was that of St. Paul's Cathedral, which rose 500 feet high from its hilltop site overlooking the City. The city walls were marked by many ancient gates, dating from medieval times – Bishopsgate, Aldgate, Cripplegate, Ludgate, Moorgate and others – and within their boundary there were some 97 parish churches, roughly one for every hundred citizens. Besides these there were "a score of great religious houses" – at least until Henry VIII dissolved them – each with its own gardens, cloisters and spire. We can easily imagine how the pealing of the church bells must have filled the air in this small community on Sundays.

A citizen and his wife on horseback

But by Tudor times London had expanded some way beyond the old city walls. Over London Bridge, dating from 1176, with its nineteen piers and wooden houses above, lay the important suburb of Southwark, prosperous and independent from the jurisdiction of the sheriffs and aldermen of the City itself. Southwark indeed was notorious for its playhouses and other forms of entertainment so often frowned upon by the City, and here, on May Days and other holidays, Londoners

Right Old St. Paul's Cathedral

Below A model of the Royal Exchange, Cornhill, London

Left Richmond Palace, built by Henry VIII

Spectators watching an archery contest in Finsbury Field, outside London

A barber's shop

would flock for a day's amusement. Along other roads leading out of London there could be seen ribbon development, the new houses and shops slowly devouring what once had been open fields and pasture land.

To many people, the growth of London seemed to threaten the well-being of the nation as a whole. As Professor Bindoff has written, "Tudor London devoured people – life in the city was so unhealthy that the population showed scarcely any natural increase but grew almost entirely by immigration; it devoured foodstuffs, pushing the tentacles of its victualling organism ever further along the coasts and up the river-valleys and raising prices wherever they penetrated." Such was the demand of the dense population, many of them with rich tables, that the county of Kent with its enclosed fields was already called "the garden of England". London's own orchard was rich with "apples beyond measure and also with cherries." Barley harvested to the north in East Anglia was brewed at Royston to quench London's thirst, while hops were brewed in Kent and Essex. Many farmers grew rich from supplying the needs of the great city. A contemporary found "another sort of husbandman, or yeoman rather, who wade in the weeds of gentlemen . . . who having great feeding for cattle" sell their fat stock at Smithfield meat market, "where also they store themselves with lean. There are also those that live by carriage for other men, and to that end they keep carts and carriages, carry milk, meal and other things to London whereby they live very gainfully."

London was proud of its civic independence. Its affairs were managed by members of the rich merchant companies. The Mercers, Grocers, Drapers, Fishmongers and Goldsmiths, for example, produced nearly all the mayors and aldermen of early Tudor London. These were men who owed their wealth, not to feudal inheritances, but to their thriving export trade pushed to all parts of the known world, principally of corn, wool and finished cloth. The wharves of the River Thames were filled with their ships, whose forest of masts formed a counterpart to the forest of spires within the city walls.

These merchants had avoided entanglement with either the Yorkist or Lancastrian contenders for the English crown during the Wars of the Roses, and had concentrated instead on building their own mercantile power, displayed in the ever-increasing pomp and circumstance of their civic processions and ceremonial.

London's pre-eminence in the nation's affairs was due in part to the fact that it was the centre of the legal system. Since the time of Magna Carta in 1215, the Court of Common Pleas was fixed at Westminster. This was the court where one subject could bring an action against another to settle a property dispute, judges' and lawyers' chambers were concentrated near Chancery Lane, or Chancellor's Lane as it was originally known. Near at hand were the Inns of Court where the law students had their homes, including Gray's Inn, the Middle Temple and Inner Temple, Furnival's Inn and Baynard's Inn, and others.

Alien townsfolk

Symbolic of the growing sense of national pride manifested in the towns was a resurgence of hostility towards aliens. This hostility, indeed, had a long history. An Italian wrote in 1497, for example, "Londoners have such fierce tempers and wicked dispositions that they not only despise the way in which Italians live, but actually pursue them with uncontrolled hatred. They look askance at us by day, and at night they sometimes drive us off with sticks and blows of the truncheon." Italians were particularly disliked by some Englishmen, at least, because of Italian dominance in English religious affairs as expressed by the papacy; and the annual tribute of "Peter's Pence" payable to the Pope was singled out for special attack (although this was ended during Henry VIII's Reformation).

All aliens had to register themselves, and pay a punitive tax of forty shillings a year if they were householders. Many of them tried to avoid registering. But despite local hostility, the number of registered aliens rose from about 500 in the mid-fifteenth century to more than 5,000 by Queen Elizabeth I's reign. The aliens made a valuable contribution to English life, by bringing with them new ideas and exotic merchandise from Europe and further afield. This unnamed English poet, however, had little time for foreign ways:

> The great galleys of Venice and Florence
> Be well laden with things of complaisance [pleasure],
> All spicerie and other grocer's ware,
> With sweet wines, all manner of chaffare,
> Apes and japes and marmusets tailed,
> Nifles, trifles that little have availed,
> And things with which they featly bleare our eye,
> With things not enduring that we buy.

Many townsmen were happy enough to live and work with European aliens, who often brought trade, or payment for lodgings. But most foreigners found that London's inhabitants are "extremely proud and overbearing, and because the greater part, especially the tradespeople, seldom go into other countries, but always remain in their houses in the city attending to their business, they care little for foreigners, but scoff

A merchant in the sixteenth century

Above left Weighing minerals

Above A wealthy merchant of London wearing fine clothes

Left Queen Elizabeth's coaches

Below Metallurgy: men and their tools

and laugh at them." A Frenchman called Stephen Perlin dismissed Londoners in 1558 as given "only to vanity and ambition, and to all sorts of merchandise."

Occasionally, as in 1517, hostility towards the alien community erupted into open violence. In that year the apprentices began to roam the streets and harass aliens until the authorities thought it prudent to impose a curfew from nine o'clock at night until seven in the morning on the eve of May Day – the traditional season for drunken brawls among the apprentices. As often happened with no police force, the authorities over-reacted when the curfew was broken. Shots were fired, volunteers from the Inns of Court were summoned, and several arrests were made. Then, at a special court convened on 4th May several boys – "poor younglings" barely in their teens – were hanged forthwith, to the consternation of their distracted parents. But others were pardoned by the King, and the gallows were dismantled. But the people of London had had a foretaste of the judicial barbarity that was to become commonplace in the rest of the Tudor period.

Wooden carving on the facade of
a London house

A clasp maker

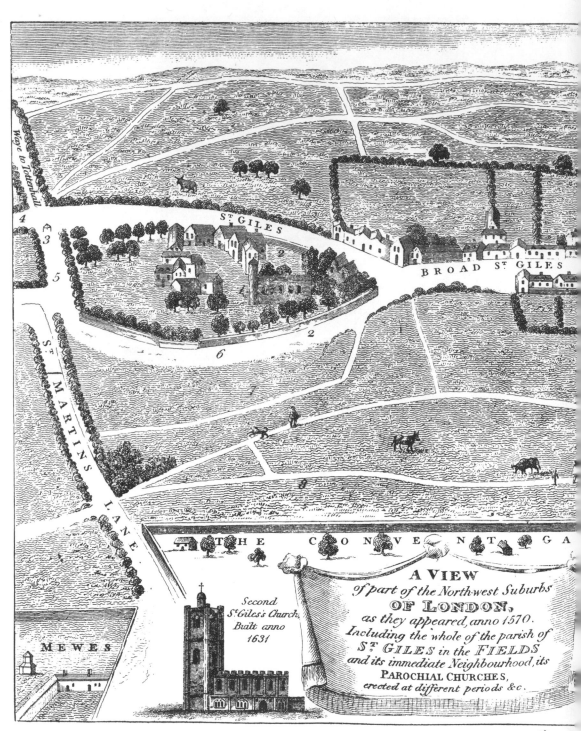

A VIEW
of part of the North-west Suburbs
OF LONDON,
as they appeared, anno 1570.
Including the whole of the parish of
St GILES in the FIELDS
and its immediate Neighbourhood, its
PAROCHIAL CHURCHES,
erected at different periods &c.

Second
St Giles's Church,
Built anno
1631

THE PARISH OF St Giles

The part of the North West Suburbs of London, since called Saint Giles's, was about the time of
habitations.—— The parish derived its name if not its origin from the ancient Hospital for
and dedicated to Saint Giles: before which time there had been only a small Chapel
and dwellings in the flourishing times of Saint Giles's Hospital, but declined in popu-
inconsiderable village till the end of the reign of Elizabeth, after which period it was
The great increase of St Giles's Parish occasioned the separation of St Georges
by the great Plan of London by Ralph Aggas, and partly from authorities for-

The Seal of the Amb

A view of London: in Tudor times much of London was open fields

Men carrying a sedan

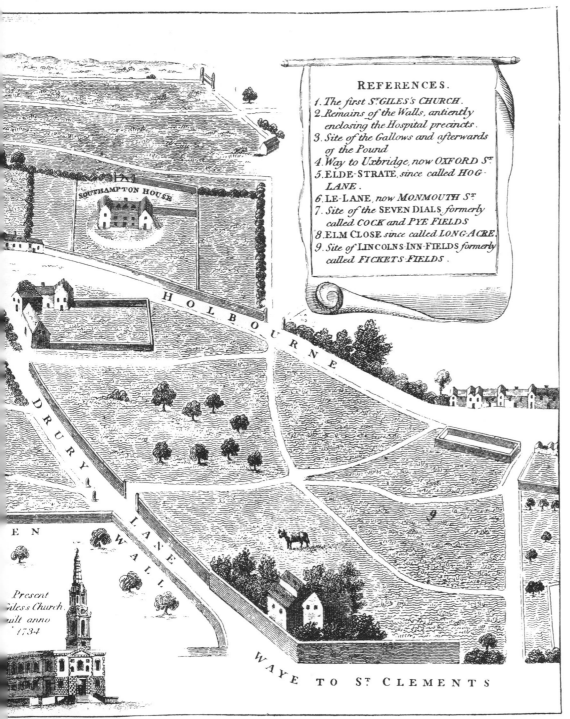

SOUTHAMPTON HOUSE

HOLBOURNE

DRURY LANE WALL

Present
...iles Church
...ilt anno
1734

WAYE TO St CLEMENTS

...tel of St Giles

REFERENCES.

1. *The first* St GILES'S CHURCH.
2. *Remains of the Walls, antiently enclosing the Hospital precincts.*
3. *Site of the Gallows and afterwards of the Pound*
4. *Way to Uxbridge, now* OXFORD St.
5. ELDE-STRATE, *since called* HOG-LANE.
6. LE-LANE, *now* MONMOUTH St.
7. *Site of the* SEVEN DIALS *formerly called* COCK *and* PYE FIELDS
8. ELM CLOSE *since called* LONG-ACRE.
9. *Site of* LINCOLNS-INN-FIELDS *formerly called* FICKETS-FIELDS.

in the Fields. LONDON.

the Norman Conquest an un-built tract of country, or but thinly scattered with Lepers; which was built on the site of the present church, by MATILDA queen of King Henry I. or ...zary on the Spot. — It is described in old records, as abounding with gardens ...lation and buildings after the suppression of that establishment, and remained but an rapidly built on, and became distinguished for the number and rank of its inhabitants. Bloomsbury Parish from it anno 1734. — The above view (which is partly supplied ...nished by parochial documents,) was taken anno 1570.

Sovereigns (gold coins) showing Henry VIII and the Tudor rose

Above left The Lord Mayor of London talking to his aldermen.
Right Merchants' wives and a countrywoman

Crime in the towns

The problem of crime was, indeed, a serious one in Tudor towns. The treatment of offenders was, to a modern observer, unbelievably severe. In this great age of religious upheaval, heretics were burned at the stake; cutpurses, coin-clippers and "conny catchers" (tricksters) were hanged; traitors were hung, drawn and quartered; and smalltime offenders and vagrants were whipped at the cart tail, pilloried, or put in the stocks. In his book *Utopia* (1516), Sir Thomas More thought that "this punishment of thieves passeth the limits of justice, and it also very hurtful to the weal-public [public well-being]. For it is too extreme and cruel a punishment for theft, and yet not sufficient to refrain and withhold men from theft. . . . No man should be driven to this extreme necessity, first to steal and then to die."

Other people disagreed. One writer, Thomas Harman, had little time for the cunning thieves who "walk a-daytimes from house to house to demand charity" and "vigilantly mark where or in what place they may attain to their prey, casting their eyes up to every window, well noting what they see there, whether apparel or linen, hanging near unto the said windows. . . . They customarily carry with them a staff of four or five feet long, in which, within one inch of the top thereof, is a little hole bored through, in which hole they put an iron hook, and . . . pluck unto them quickly anything that they may reach therewith." (*A Caveat or Warning*, 1567).

A printing shop

Above Wheels driven by water operating the shaft of a copper mine

Below Minting coins

These are some typical punishments meted out by the courts in the time of Elizabeth I:

"Agnes Osier, alias Beggar, of Brook Street in South Weald, spinster, for breaking into the house of William Reynolds of the same in the night time, and stealing two flaxen sheets worth 4s. 4d. and 60s. in money, belonging to the said William. Guilty, to be hanged." (Essex, 1599).

"Thomas Boteworth is fined four pence because he is a common brawler and disturber of his neighbours, and to give him warning to leave it, or else he is to be carried in a dung cart about the town in open assembly, and then to be put into the stocks and then to be banished out of the lordship." (Essex, 1558).

"The wife of Walter Hycosks and the wife of Peter Phillips do be common scolds, and therefore it is ordered that they shall be admonished thereof in the church, to leave their scolding. But upon complaint made by their neighbours the second time they shall be punished by the ducking stool according to the direction of the constable." (Essex, 1592).

In his *Travels in England* (1599) Thomas Platter noted how the populace thronged into London each quarter as the law courts went into session. "Everything is saved up until that time, then there is a slaughtering and a hanging." And from all the prisons people were taken out and tried, and when the trials were over, those condemned to the rope were carted off by the hangman to the place of public execution at Tyburn. There, the hangman "fastens them up one after another by

Above A baker taking loaves out of his oven

Below People who committed crimes were likely to be put in the stocks *below* or locked in a pillory *bottom*

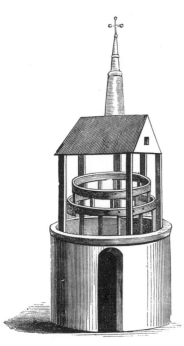

the rope, and drives the cart off under the gallows, which is not very high off the ground. Then the criminal's friends come and draw them down by their feet, that they may die all the sooner."

The punishment for brawling within the precincts of the Court was notably severe, although it was seldom imposed. Sir Edmund Knevet, for example, was sentenced to the loss of his right hand in 1541. It had been necessary to summon the following officers to carry out the sentence:

1. The sergeant-surgeon, with his surgical instruments;
2. The sergeant of the woodyard with a mallet and block;
3. The master-cook with a suitable knife;
4. The sergeant of the larder, as an authority on carving;
5. The sergeant-farrier with hot irons to cauterize the wound;
6. The yeoman of the chandlery with bandages to bind the wound;
7. The yeoman of the scullery with a pan of fire to heat the cautery irons, and a dish of cold water to cool the ends of the irons where they were to be held;
8. The sergeant of the cellar with wine and ale, presumably for sustaining the unfortunate prisoner;
9. The yeoman of the ewery with basins and towels for those who wished to wash.

Fortunately for Sir Edmund, Henry VIII lifted the sentence at the last minute. The prisoner had requested that his left hand be cut off, "for if my right hand be spared, I may hereafter do such service to his Grace as shall please him to appoint."

Those cast into prison were less fortunate. Most of them were sentenced for debt, and their only hope of release was to have their debts paid by their family or friends. But the expenses of remaining in gaol could be so great – prisoners had to supply their own food and comforts – that this hope soon disappeared for many.

In his *Anatomy of Abuses* (1585) Stubbes complained strongly of conditions in prison. "Believe me, it grieveth me to hear – walking in the streets – the pitiful cries and miserable complaints of poor prisoners in durance [hardship] for debt, and likely so to continue all their life, destitute of liberty, meat, drink (though of the meanest sort), and clothing to their backs, lying in filthy straw and loathsome dung, worse than any dog, void of all charitable consolation and brotherly comfort in this world, wishing and thirsting after death, to set them at liberty and loose them from their shackles."

As Andrew Borde noted in his *Breviary of Health* (1547) many prison inmates fell foul of "gaol fever". "This infirmity doth come of corruption of the air, and of the breath and filth which doth come from men, as many men be together in a little room having but little open air." Borde was not very sanguine about the remedy: "The chief remedy is for man so to live and so to do that he deserve not to be brought into no prison. And if he be in prison, either to get friends to help him out, or else to use some perfumes or to smell some odorous savours, and to keep the person clean."

It was indeed a gloomy prospect for those who, whether due to

Above A man making scales

Top A man weaving cloth on a loom and *bottom* A brewer pouring beer into barrels

Above A night watchman carrying a torch to light up the streets.

Below A blacksmith making horseshoes

Below A butcher and his servant

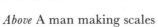
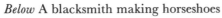

A London haberdasher selling
hats and stockings

A Tudor man making a magnet

Craftsmen hammering metal to
make coins

impoverishment or criminality, fell foul of the harsh Tudor judicial
system.

Violent pleasures

In an age of sudden death, injustice and hardship, it is scarcely sur-
prising that the most popular entertainments were sometimes the
cruellest. A fascinating account of bear and bull baiting was written
by Thomas Platter in his *Travels in England* (1599): "Every Sunday
and Wednesday in London there are bear-baitings . . . The theatre is
circular, with galleries round the top for the spectators, the ground
space down below, beneath the clear sky, is unoccupied. In the middle
of this place a large bear on a long rope was bound to a stake, then a
number of great English mastiffs were brought in and shown first to the
bear, which they afterwards baited one after another: now the excellence
and fine temper of such mastiffs was evinced, for although they were
much struck and mauled by the bear, they did not give in, but had to
be pulled off by sheer force, and their muzzles forced open with long
sticks to which a broad ironpiece was attached at the top. The bear's
teeth were not sharp so they could not injure the dogs; they have them
broken short. When the first mastiffs tired, fresh ones were brought in
to bait the bear.

"When the first bear was weary, another one was supplied and fresh
dogs to bait him, first one at a time, then more and more as it lasted,
till they had overpowered the bear, then only did they come to its aid.
This second bear was very big and old, and kept the dogs at bay so
artfully with his paws that they could not score a point off him until
there were more of them. When this bear was tired, a large white

Firemen putting out a fire with one of the first fire engines

A coppersmith making different objects from copper

powerful bull was brought in, and likewise bound in the centre of the theatre, and one dog only was set on him at a time, which he speared with his horns and tossed in such masterly fashion, that they could not get the better of him, and as the dogs fell to the floor again, several men held the sticks under them to break their fall, so that they would not be killed. Afterwards more dogs were set on him, but could not down him. Then another powerful bear was fetched and baited by six or seven dogs at a time, which attacked him bravely on all sides, but could not get the better of him because of his thick pelt.

"Lastly they brought in an old blind bear which the boys hit with canes and sticks; but he knew how to untie his leash and he ran back to his stall."

Left A goldsmith's workshop

4 *The Tudor Home*

WITH THE ENDING of the long period of strife and civil war of the Wars of the Roses, Englishmen began to feel more security in their daily lives. As the years of Tudor rule unfolded, people looked more to the comfort of their homes. They began to design them as places of pleasure and relaxation, and the fortified houses of earlier times were less often built. By the reign of Elizabeth (1558–1603), the years of peace at home, and the prosperity of English commerce, meant that the nation as a whole enjoyed a higher standard of living than it had ever known.

House and home

For centuries, English houses had been built on the timber-frame principle. Oak was commonly used for the upright joists, or "studs". The spaces in between were filled up with wattle and daub, and plastered over. Sometimes, bricks would be used instead of wattle. This method was known as brick-nogging.

In 1587, William Harrison noted: "The ancient manors and houses of our gentlemen are yet, and for the most part, of strong timber, in framing whereof our carpenters have been and are worthily preferred before those of like science among all other nations." More recently built houses "are commonly either of brick or hard stone, or both; their rooms large and comely, and houses of office further distant from their lodgings. Those of the nobility are likewise wrought with brick and hard stone, as provision may be best made."

One reason why bricks were used more often was that timber was growing scarce, consumed in great quantities for house and ship building, and for charcoal burning. In many areas, the felling of timber was actually forbidden or restricted. In the words of a proclamation, "There hath been such consumption of timber in the realm that in the very City of London they are now driven to build with beech and other timber of small continuance [life], which in time will be to the notorious peril and decay of the city. It is now commanded that no part of a tree that may serve for any use of timber shall be converted to coal or firewood. And for the better preservation of timber, from the feast of St. Michael no one shall erect any new house . . . except all outer walls and windows be made wholly of brick, or brick and stone."

Opposite: above Tudor homes often had oak beamed ceilings and heavy oak furniture. *Below* A panelled room in a wealthy Tudor house

A helmet worn by a Tudor knight

There were few architects in the modern sense. For a large house the plans were often drawn up by a master mason. He and his workmen built the shell of the house. The master carpenter managed internal details such as walls, ceilings and fireplaces. In his diary the Earl of Cork records his discussions with the craftsmen who were decorating his new home: "I have agreed with Christopher Watts, freemason and carver, who dwells in Horse Street, Bristol, to make me a very fair chimney, also for my parlour, which is to reach up close to the ceiling, with my coat of arms complete, with crest, helmet, coronet, supporters, mantling and footpace, which he is to set up and finish all at his own charges, fair and graceful in all respects, and for that chimney I am to pay £10, and I am to find carriage also. He is also to make twelve figures each three foot high, to set upon my staircase for which he demands 20s. apiece, and I offer him 13s. 4d.* And he is presently to cut one of them with the figure of Pallas with a shield. One with a coat with a coronet to be cut for a trial."

The eminent educationalist Sir Andrew Borde outlined his idea of a perfect home: "Make the hall under such a fashion, that the parlour be annexed to the head of the hall. And the buttery and pantry to be at the lower end of the hall, the cellar under the pantry . . . the kitchen set somewhat a-base from the buttery and pantry . . . the pantry house and the larder house annexed to the kitchen . . . Let the private chamber be annexed to the chamber of estate, with other chambers necessary for the building so that many of the chambers may have a prospect into the Chapel . . . The bake house and brew house should be a distance from . . . other buildings."

An interesting description of a house and its contents appears in a will made by Thomas Quenel of Lythe Hill, Chiddingford, who died in 1571: "Item, I give and bequeath to Agnes my wife enduring the time of her natural life my parlour in the west side of my house at Lythehill which adjoins the hall there, the chamber over the same parlour, the garret above the same chamber, the loft over the hall, and the kitchen loft with free ingress, egress and regress. Room and fire in the said hall at all times, and half the kitchen, and firewood to dress meat and drink, bake and brew, and to do all other necessaries meet and convenient in the same kitchen at all times and half the new coop now standing in the said kitchen."

Thomas also left his wife, outside the house itself, "all my old stable which adjoineth to the west side of my house, the west end of my range [barn] to lay hay or straw in, and half the rest of my range, and also the upper gates for her cattles [and] all my herber [garden] which adjoineth to the east side of my said house. And all my orchard which adjoineth to the said herber on the south side of my said house from the new pale that adjoineth unto the said herber on the east side unto the home field on the west side, and extendeth from the said house on the north side unto the little mead on the south side."

The Tudors were great gardeners. The houses of the rich had splendid garths (gardens), and sometimes deer parks. The gardens were laid out Italian-style with geometrically arranged paths and walks, with flowerbeds and shrubs between. The garden was usually overlooked

Tennis was played in Tudor times on enclosed courts

* £1 = 20 shillings, one shilling was equal to 12 pence.

Opposite The Great Hall in a nobleman's mansion

Right Many kitchen boys were employed to prepare the meals for a noble family

from a stone terrace in front of the house. At the royal palace of Hampton Court, Thomas Platter noticed by the entrance, "numerous patches where square cavities had been scooped out, as for paving stones. Some of these were filled with red brick dust, some with white sand, and some with green lawn, very much resembling a chess board. The hedges and surrounds were of hawthorn, bush firs, ivy, roses, juniper, holly, English or common elm, box and other shrubs, very gay and attractive."

Sir Andrew Borde considered it "a commodious and a pleasant thing" for a mansion to have an orchard. But "it is more commodious to have a fair garden, repleted with herbs of aromatick and redolent savours. . . . Also a park replete with deer and conyes [rabbits] is a necessary and pleasant thing to be annexed to a mansion. A dove house is also a necessary thing about a mansion place. And among other things a pair of butts is a decent thing . . . . And other while for a great man necessary it is for to pass his time with bowls in an alley." (*A Compendious Regiment*, 1567).

Such gardens and orchards were a sign of peaceful and prosperous times. One garden contained a pyramid of marble, full of concealed

Little Moreton Hall in Cheshire is a magnificent example of
Tudor domestic architecture with its wonderfully designed oak
beams and whitewashed plaster. A notable feature of Tudor
homes was their windows which let in far more light than in
medieval times

The Chariott drawne by foure Horses vpon which Charret stood the Coffin couered with purple Veluett and vpon that the representation. The Canapy borne by six Knights.

Opposite The Cholmondeley Sisters. A charming painting of twin sisters with their children. The characteristic severity of style is softened by the evident pleasure taken in its domestic content

Below The funeral procession of Queen Elizabeth I in 1603. "The most resplendeth sun setteth at last in a western cloud." Queen Elizabeth had reigned for forty-five years; under her firm rule England had achieved economic and maritime strength and also social stability. The passing of "Gloriana", as this last Tudor monarch was often known, was deeply mourned by most of her subjects

Left Mary Arden's cottage in Wilmcote, Warwickshire, with timber frame construction and leaded windows

Right A dispensary, which belonged to Dr. Hall, at Hall's Croft, Stratford-upon-Avon, the town of Shakespeare's birth. This typical Tudor interior shows a wooden-beamed ceiling. The room contains the doctor's pots in which he kept his medicines and herbs, and also his mortars and pestles

Far right This is the parlour in Hall's Croft, lit today by electric light, but in Dr. Hall's time by wax candles. The heavy oak furniture is in keeping with the architecture of the building

Opposite This beautiful painting depicts the civilized quality of life in which the Tudors took such pleasure. On the opposite side of the River Thames can be seen the majestic towers of Richmond Palace. Tudor gentlemen in cloaks and ruffs are rowed sedately up and down the River by the watermen enjoying the scene with its fine brick and stone houses, gardens, and swans. Morris dancers are in the foreground, one of whom is collecting money from a gentleman and his lady who have probably alighted from the fine covered coach

Right A splendid contemporary painting of the great conflict between the English navy and the Armada of Philip II's Spain in 1558. Francis Drake had "singed the King of Spain's beard" by his daring raid on Cadiz. The defeat of the Armada, in the longest naval engagement ever recorded at that time, set the seal on England's maritime power for generations to come

pipes, "which spirt upon all who come within their reach." The Tudors loved mechanical ingenuity and trickery of this kind. William Harrison found a variety of fruits – many of them new to England – grown in English orchards towards the end of Queen Elizabeth's reign – apples, plums, pears, walnuts, filberts, apricots, almonds, peaches, figs, corn trees, capers, oranges, lemons. Many of these were first shipped from Italy in the time of Henry VIII. Some, like rhubarb, were grown for their medicinal properties.

Opposite: George Clifford, the third Duke of Cumberland (1558–1605)

In the Tudor period there were no electric lights so candles were used. Many candles could be held in a chandelier

E

A wooden chest in which a young girl stored her dowry

Many writers noted the increase in comfort – some, Puritan in outlook, disapprovingly. Walls inside the houses of noblemen and merchants were frequently panelled in oak, and the panels themselves hung with rich tapestries, or with severe-looking family portraits. The ceilings were often decorated with fine stucco work. The chimney breasts were elaborately carved, and woven rush mats lay on the floor in place of the messier loose rushes more common in Henry VIII's day. Although chairs were still rare, and baths unknown, benches and settles might be upholstered for greater comfort.

William Harrison wrote that in noblemen's houses it was no longer rare to see rich hangings of tapestry, silver vessels, and as much plate as would fill two or three cupboards, worth as much as one or two thousand pounds. Likewise, in the houses of knights and gentlemen, merchants and other wealthy citizens, a visitor might expect to find "great provision of tapistrie, Turkis worke, pewter, brasse, fine linen, and thereto costlie cupbords of plate . . . ." Independent farmers and master craftsmen, too, were filling their cupboards with plate, draping their solid oak beds with tapestry and even silk hangings, their tables with fine napkins. Tin and pewter were more often used for plates and cutlery, replacing the crude wooden or earthenware utensils of previous generations.

In his *History of the Netherlands* (1575) the Dutch writer Van Meteren found that wives in England were entirely in the power of their husbands, only their lives excepted. He found it odd that when they married they should give up their father's family surname and adopt that of their husbands. Only duchesses, countesses and baronesses were allowed to

Right Two boys from a noble family playing a game of bowls

A sixteenth-century clock

Die Venerilla mihi, quis sit magé conus amænus
Optimus est medius, sic ego vera loquor.

Zart Schön Jungfraw ich euch fragn will
Welchr ist der best Kegel im Spiell.
Herr so ich euch soll sagen feinn,
So solls der Mittel Kegel seinn. 9

keep their own names when marrying men of lower rank. Even this practice, he said, was tolerated rather than approved. "Yet they are not kept so strictly as they are in Spain or elsewhere . . . but have the free management of the house or housekeeping, after the fashion of those of the Netherlands, and others their neighbours. They go to market to buy what they like best to eat. They are well-dressed, fond of taking it easy, and commonly leave the care of household matters and drudgery to their servants."

Indeed, the state of bondage to which Van Meteren referred had its compensations. English ladies sat before their doors, "decked out in fine cloths, in order to see and be seen by the passers-by. In all banquets and feasts they are shown the greatest honours. They are placed at the upper end of the table, where they are first served; at the lower end they help the men. All the rest of the time they employ in walking and riding, in playing at cards or otherwise, in visiting their friends and keeping company, conversing with their equals (whom they term 'gossips') and their neighbours, and making merry with them at child-births, christenings, churchings and funerals – and all this with the permissions and knowledge of their husbands, as such is the custom. . . . This is why England is called the paradise of married women."

Meals

In a great Tudor house, especially by the time of Elizabeth, meals were long and elaborate. Breakfast was generally dispensed with, but dinner, served just before noon, would often last two or three hours. Supper

A pewter dish and jugs

Left Tudor household utensils made of earthenware

Below left Rich Tudor people slept in carved wooden four-poster beds like the Great Bed of Ware

Below A maidservant smoothing out sheets with a stick

67

A farmer's wife weaving yarn into cloth on a loom

was eaten at about six o'clock, before the darkness necessitated candles. All the members of the family who were at home would be at table together with their guests and friends. Guests of lower social position, such as the boys' tutors, would normally sit at the lower end of the long table.

The wife of a Tudor nobleman active in state affairs always had to be ready to entertain a large number of visitors. Her store cupboard would be filled with barrels of salted meat and fish, and spices and delicacies such as cloves, ginger, maces, figs, raisins, hops, honey, oil, vinegar, salt, almonds, dates, saffron and cinnamon. She would also keep a store of pastries and cakes, as well as home-made jellies of many different kinds, and ales and wines, ciders and perries.

Here is an account by one Gilbert Walker, in 1532, of a visit to a friend's house in London. "The table was fair spread with diaper cloths, the cupboard garnished with much goodly plate, and last of all came forth the gentlewoman his wife, clothed in silks and embroidered works." Her headdress was "broidered with gold and pearl." A carcanet was about her neck, with a flower of diamonds pendant, and fair rings on her finger. " 'Bess,' quoth he, 'bid this gentleman welcome.' And with that she courteously kissed me. . . . I saw not a woman in all my life whose fashions and entertainments I liked better." Gilbert's host then brought him through "divers well-trimmed chambers, the worst of

An Elizabethan masque: an elaborate entertainment which involved music and dancing

Opposite: top A farmer's wife spinning wool into yarn.
Below The Lady Mayoress of London

69

A Tudor wedding feast. The guests are having a wonderful time dancing, feasting and making music

Above Tudor noblemen had enormous meals which lasted several hours
Below A Tudor lady wearing a high ruff and a farthingale skirt

them apparelled with verdures, some with rich cloth of arras, all with beds, chairs and cushions of silk and gold, of sundry colours, suitably wrought. 'Lo here,' quoth he, 'a poor man's lodging. . . .' "

As one of the seven deadly sins, gluttony did not inhibit the Tudors from indulging themselves at table. At the end of a meal, the leftovers would be distributed among the servants and the poor. In the reign of Queen Mary, a Spanish visitor remarked, "These English have themselves houses made of sticks and dirt, but they fare commonly so well as the King!" Harrison's answer was, "Coarse fare in rude cabins is better than their own thin diet in princely habitations!" – not that the homes of the Tudor gentry could often by called "rude cabins".

Things were very different in the poorest homes. No roasting spits, sieves, kneading troughs, fire shovels and chafing-dishes there – just a crude knife, and a piece of bread to serve as a platter. A peasant farm-worker would be glad to get a meal of bread and rye, some bacon, thin milk, curds, with perhaps a little locally-brewed beer or cider. If his family had any pots and dishes, they would not be made of silver plate, Venetian glass or pewter, but rough earthenware.

William Harrison wrote in 1577, "the bread throughout our land is made of such grain as the soil yieldeth; nevertheless the gentility commonly provide themselves sufficiently of wheat for their own tables, whilst their own household and poor neighbours in some shires are forced to content themselves with rye or barley, yea and in time of dearth many with bread made out of beans, peason, or oats and some

Left A banquet in a great hall

Below A man offering food to a traveller. *Bottom* A farmer's wife churning butter

acorns among." Around the end of the Tudor period, the traveller and writer Fynes Moryson wrote: "The English husbandmen eat barley and rye brown bread, and prefer it to white bread as abiding longer in the stomach, and not so soon digested with their labour. But citizens and gentlemen eat most pure white bread. . .

"The English have abundance of white meats, of all kinds of flesh, fowl, fish and things good for food. In the seasons of the year the English eat fallow deer plentifully, as bucks in summer and does in winter, which they bake in pasties, and this venison pasty is a dainty, rarely found in any other kingdom. England, yea perhaps one county thereof, hath more fallow deer than all Europe that I have seen. No kingdom of the world hath so many dove-houses. Likewise, brawn is a proper meat to the English, not known to others. English cooks, in comparison with other nations, are most commended for roast meats."

A modern visitor would have thought little of Tudor table manners at any level of society. There were no forks on the table, just a knife and spoon. The men wore their hats at table and belched noisily. Empty drinking glasses were returned to a sideboard to be wiped clean by a servant before being used by other guests. But to the Englishman, the main thing was to eat and drink well. Tudor banquets were noted for the richness and variety of the food – the meats served at one meal might include beef, mutton, lamb, veal, kid, pork, coney, capon, pig, venison, domestic fowl and wildfowl.

These verses written in 1577 by Hugh Rhodes in his *Book of Nurture*, *or Schole of Good Maners* give children and servants instructions on how to behave at table:

Looke that your knyfe be sharp & kene to cut your
  meate withall;
So the more cleanlyer, be sure, cut your meate you
  shall.
Or thou put much bread in thy pottage, looke thou
  doe it assay;
Fill not they spoone to full, least thou loose
  somewhat by the way.

And sup not lowde of they Pottage, no tyme in all
  thy lyfe:
Dip not thy meate in the Saltseller, but take it
  with thy knyfe.
When thou haste eaten thy Pottage, doe as I shall
  thee wish:
Wype clean thy spone, I do thee read, leave it not
  in the dish;
Lay it downe before thy trenchoure, thereof be not
  afrayde;
And take heede who takes it up, for feare it be
  convayde.
Cut not the best peece for thyselfe, leave thou some
  parte behynde:
Bee not greedye of meate and drinke; be liberall and
  kynde.
Burnish no bones with thy teeth, for that is unseemely;
Rend not thy meate asunder, for that swarves from
  curtesy;
And if a stranger syt neare thee, ever among now and
  than
Reward thou him with some daynties: shew thyselfe a
  Gentleman.
If your fellow sit from his meate and cannot come
  thereto,
Then cutte for him such as thou haste; he may lyke
  for thee doe.
Scratche not thy head with thy fyngers when thou
  arte at thy meate;
Nor spytte you over the table boorde — see thou doest
  not this forget.
Pick not thy teeth with thy Knyfe nor with thy
  fyngers ende,
But take a stick, or some cleane thyng, then doe
  you not offende.

Fyll not thy mouth to full, leaste thou perhaps of
  force must speake;
Nor blow not out thy crums when thou doest eate.
Fowle not the place with spitting whereas thou doest
  syt,
Leaste it abhore some that syt by: let reason rule
  thy wyt.

Opposite: above Servants in the kitchen preparing a feast for the lords and ladies who are dancing in the great hall. *Below* A countrywoman cooking food over an open fire

A sixteenth century table

A four-poster bed. The curtains could be drawn to keep out draughts

The same author gave advice to servants on how to wait at table: "When your Master will go to his meat, take a towel about your neck, then take a cupboard cloth, a basin, ewer, and a towel, to array your cupboard: cover your table, set on bread, salt and trenchers, the salt before the bread, and trenchers before the salt. Set your napkins and spoons on the cupboard ready, and lay every man a trencher, a napkin, and a spoon. And if you have more messes than one at your master's table, consider what degree they be of, and thereafter you may serve them: and then set down everything at that mess as before, except your carving knives.

"If there be many gentlemen or yeomen, then set on bread, salt, trenchers and spoons, after they be seated, or else after the custom of the house . . . . See you have voyders ready for to avoid [empty away] the morsels that they do leave on their trenchers. Then with your trencher knife take of such fragments, and put them in your voyder, and set them down clean again. . . .

"Then take up the salt, and make obeisance; and mark if your master use to wash at the table, or standing. If he be at the table, cast a clean towel on your table cloth, and set down your basin and ewer before your sovereign, and take the ewer in your hand, and give them water. Then void your basin and ewer, and fold the board cloth, together with your towel therein, and so take them of the board. And when your sovereign shall wash, set your towel on the left hand of him, and the water before your sovereign at dinner or supper. If it be to bedward, set up your basin and towel on the cupboard again."

A great noble establishment such as Hatfield House would have scores of servants to undertake the domestic duties. Among them might be a few page boys, the young sons of good family who in the sixteenth and seventeenth century were recruited for domestic duties in return for free clothing, bed and board. This verse, reproduced from *The Young Children's Book* of about 1500 gives the following advice:

Arise betymme oute of thy bed
And blesse thy brest and thy forehead
Then washe thy hands and then thy face,
Comb thy head and ask God grace
Thee to help in all thy works;
Thou shall speed better what so thou carpes
Then go to church and hear a mass,
There ask mercy for thy trespass.
To whom thou mightest come by the way
Courteously "good morning" thou might say,
When thou hast done go break thy fast
With meat and drink of good repast.
Bless thy mouth ere it shall eat
The better shall be thy diet.
Before thy meat say thou thy grace,
It occupies but little space.

It was important to see that the right kind of servants were taken into the family, and to take heed "howe yee put them in authorytye among

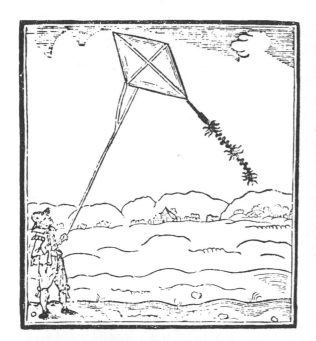

If on your man you light
The first draught shall you play,
If not 'tis mine by right
At first to lead the way

Ioannes Stradanus Inuent.

P Furnius

Top left Boys enjoyed many of the same games they do today. *Right*
A game of chess. *Below* The ladies of a noble household were
taught to do fine embroidery

Above The English gentlewoman
(1631) *left* and the English
gentleman (1633) *right*
Below left A Tudor lady's shoe.
Centre The type of shoe which was
worn at the end of the sixteenth
century and *right* a leather hat
covered in velvet

The tall copotain hat worn in
Queen Elizabeth's time.

A hat worn by yeomen of the
Guard

Clothes worn by an Elizabethan nobleman and his lady

your children." Parents were warned not to give their children "sumptuous apparel, for it increaseth pryde and obstinacye and many other evils."

Rhodes went on, "Take heed they speke no wordes of villanye . . . and see that they use honest sportes and games. Marke well what vyce they are inclined unto and breake it betymes." He advised them to take them often to church, and to encourage them to read the Bible and other devotional books, and equally to avoid reading "fayned fables, vayne fantasyes and wanton stories and songs of love which bring much mischiefe to youth." Little wonder that the faces of Tudor children staring down from the dark painted boards of the period commonly look so solemn and sad.

Male dress

The Tudor period is characterized by a remarkable flamboyance in dress, of men as well as women. Many writers, especially those who were Puritan in outlook, complained of the peacock dress of men, partly because it was self indulgent and partly because it tended to blur important social distinctions. In his *Anatomy of Abuses* (1585) Philip Stubbes said that it was becoming difficult to classify people according to their clothes. "Now there is such a confused mingle-mangle of apparel . . . as everyone is permitted to flaunt it out in what apparel he lusteth himself, or can get by any kind of means. So that it is very hard to know who is noble, who is worshipful, who is a gentleman, who is not. For they go daily in silks, velvets, satins, damaskes, taffetas, and suchlike, notwithstanding that they be both base by birth, mean by estate, and servile by calling."

We must thank Stubbes, as a critic, for giving us a fascinating if idiosyncratic account of male Tudor dress: "Gentlemen wore their hats sometimes on the crown of head, pearking up like the spear, or shaft of a steeple." Others wore them flat and broad on the crown "like the battlements of a house." Stubbes found both the styles and the materials used for hats "rare and straunge" – velvet, taffeta, silk, sarcenet, and wool. The characteristic Tudor ruffle was "great and monstrous", made of cambric, holland, lawn or cloth, often made a quarter of a yard deep. In Stubbes' view, Satan "first invented these great ruffs", which were held in place by starch and by a wire device known as a supportasse or underpropper. Shirts were made of materials similar to ruffs, and were "wrought throughout with needlework of silk and suchlike, and curiously stitched with open seam, and many other knacks beside, more than I can describe."

The doublets typical of the later Tudor period were "no less monstrous than the rest," hanging down the middle of the thigh. They were so stiffly quilted, "stuffed, bombasted, and sewed" as the wearer could neither work nor relax in them because they were so hot to wear. Sometimes they could "very hardly either stoop or decline to the ground, so stiff and sturdy they stand about them." They were very ornate, too, "slashed, jagged, cut, carved, pinked and laced with all kinds of costly lace of divers and sundry colours. . . ."

A young Elizabethan gentleman wearing doublet and hose

Sixteenth-century daggers

A sixteenth-century sword

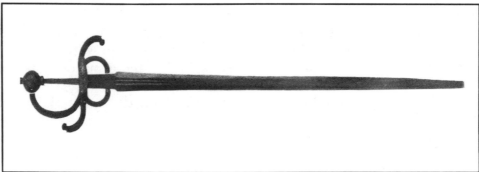

But the Tudors did not entirely neglect practical considerations in dress. One Sir Hugh Platt had this idea for a simple raincoat: "This garment will not be much dearer than our ordinary riding clokes. It may be made as light or lighter than our usual garments. A cloke may be prepared in such a manner, as that notwithstanding a continual rain, it shall not grow much more ponderous, than it was being dry.

"This is done by putting a sufficient quantity of Linseed oyl, mixed with Rosin, and boiled to a vernish, with Verdigrease, Vermillion, or what else you will choose to colour the same, and when you find that it is not clammy, but casts a bright colour upon a rag of cloth dipt in it, then dip therein your cloth, whereof you would make your garment, and spread it abroad and let it dry leisurely."

Sir Walter Raleigh with his son

Below An Elizabethan bride attended by her bridesmaids and watched by her friends

Stubbes remarked that no one spent more time dressing their hair, beards and moustaches than Englishmen: "There are no finer fellows under the sun, nor experter in their science of barbing than they be. They have invented such strange fashions and monstrous manners of cuttings, trimmings, shavings and washings, that you would wonder to see." When the customer came to be trimmed, he would be asked whether he wished to be cut to look fearsome to his enemy, or amiable to his friend.

"When they come to the cuttings of the hair, what snipping and snapping of scissors is there, what tricking and trimming. And when they come to washing, of how gingerly they behave themselves therein, for they have their sweet balls of soap wherewithal they use to wash. Thus come warm cloths to wipe and dry him. The last action is the payment of money, and in the end your cloak shall be brushed and – 'God be with you gentleman!' "

Women's dress

Above James I (1603–1625) holding his falcon

Women, too, came in for Stubbes's disapproval in matters of dress. For example, "They are not simply content with their own hair, but buy other hair, either of horses, mares, or any other strange beasts, dyeing it of what colour they list [please] themselves. And if there be any poor woman who hath fair hair, these nice dams will not rest till they have bought it. Or if any children have fair hair, they will entice them into a secret place and for a penny or two they will cut off their hair." On top of these "stately turrets" stood their other "capital ornaments", such as hoods and caps made of various materials – lace, taffeta, silk

Below Inflating a pig's bladder for a game of football

or wool, "according to the various phantasies of their serpentine minds."

Women, like men, wore ruffs and neckerchiefs, held in place by supportasses and underproppers, pleated and decorated and embroidered until the "ruff is the least part of itself." Stubbes added, "Sometimes they are pinned up to their ears, sometimes they are suffered to hang over their shoulders like windmill sails fluttering in the wind." Women's doublets, jerkins, cloaks and gowns were not unlike those of the menfolk, tricked out in broad ribbons and other devices. Stubbes acidly remarked that "When they have all these goodly robes upon them, women seem to be the smallest part of themselves; not . . . women of flesh and blood, but rather puppets consisting of rags and clouts compact together." And for good measure, "They must have their looking glasses carried with them wherever they go; and for good reason – for how else could they see the devil in them?"

Parson Harrison was appalled at the time and money lavished on fashions by English womenfolk: "Oh, how much cost is bestowed nowadays upon our bodies, and how little upon our souls!" He added, "How many suits of apparel hath the one, and how little furniture hath the latter! How long time is asked in decking up of the first, and how little space left wherein to feed the latter!"

All this made a tailor's life a misery: "How many times must it be sent back again to him that made it! What chafing, what fretting, what reproachful language, doth the poor workman bear away!"

The Dutch writer Van Meteren found Elizabethan women "beautiful, fair, well dressed and modest, which is seen more than elsewhere, as they go about the streets without any covering either of huke or mantle, hood, veil, or the like. Married women only wear a hat both in the street and in the house. Those unmarried go without a hat, although ladies of distinction have lately learned to cover their faces with silken masks or vizards, and feathers – for indeed they change very easily, and that every year, to the astonishment of many."

Above A young girl holding a feather fan

Below Different kinds of beard worn in Tudor times

An apothecary

5 The Breviary of Health

THE TUDORS had only a primitive knowledge of medicine. In many respects medical knowledge had hardly advanced since Chaucer's day, when the "Doctor of Physik" in *The Canterbury Tales* worked according to a complicated and superstitious system of "humours" and "complexions". Death seemed to be everywhere, unlike today where it is carefully screened from daily social life in hospitals and funeral parlours. "The Dance of Death" was a popular theme for artists of the time, in Tudor England as well as in earlier periods. Death and pestilence were so rife as often to be hardly worth attention. Preventive medicine was unknown; cures were rarely based on any scientific information, except for a thread of hit-and-miss reality in folk-medicine.

Consequently, when England – and indeed the whole of Europe – suffered the unspeakable horrors of the Black Death in the mid-fourteenth century, such a holocaust had not been outside the realm of popular imagination. From 1348 when the Black Death (the bubonic plague from Asia) first reached England, something like a third of the entire population perished in the years immediately following.

After reaping its terrible toll, however, the population of the country once more began to rise, if not in the rapid terms familiar to the modern world, at least enough for there once more to be a shortage of cultivated land for people. But even after that time, when there was an outbreak of plague in England, as happened from time to time, people resorted to prayer rather than to the physician.

An apothecary making medicine from a snake's flesh

Humours and complexions

The College of Physicians was founded in 1518, but the practice of medicine was still effectively based on the system of the ancient Greeks – a mixture of philosophy, observation and experience. The practice of medicine was founded on a belief in the four elements – Air, Fire, Water and Earth. Each had its own characteristics – cold and heat, moisture and dryness. Since man himself was a part of the natural world, the doctors believed that he shared these essential qualities, and that the special blending of them in his case produced his individual "complexion" or temperament.

For example, if heat and moisture were mixed they produced a "sanguine" man, whose humour, or characteristic, was blood. Coldness

Sixteenth-century jars used for drugs and medicines

mixed with moisture produced the phlegmatic man, whose humour was phlegm. Heat and dryness together produced the choleric type, whose humour was green or yellow bile; the melancholy man – like Robert Burton (*The Anatomy of Melancholy*) – had coldness and dryness mixed – Air and Earth. His humour was black bile. Sickness and disease were thought to be the products of an imperfect balance of the elements. Consequently, treatment consisted in an attempt to remedy the balance, using bleeding, purging, drugs and herbs, dieting, amulets or charms, and astrology.

Food, like everything else, was made up of the four elements, and its effects on the human body depended on the blending. A cabbage, for example, was characterized by hotness and dryness, and might produce choleric. Certain foods could make even a sanguine man melancholy – these included pears, apples, peaches, milk, cheese, salted meat, red deer, hare, beef, goat, peacock, pigeons, certain fish, peas, beans, dark bread, black wines, cider, perry and spices. One wonders what the effects of such foods might be on a man of naturally melancholic disposition!

Phlegmatic man, too, had to take care with his diet; indeed, diet and medicine in Tudor times were often one and the same thing. A phlegmatic man was typically "cold" and "moist". Borde (see p. 92) said, "The chief physic, the council of physicians excepted, comes from the kitchen. Therefore the physician and the cook for sick men must consult together . . . for if the doctor without the cook prepare any meal, unless he be an expert, he will make a worse dish and the patient will be unable to eat." A wealthy Tudor person suffering from fever would drink lemon containing powdered pearls. Yet diets in Tudor times were probably no more eccentric than those used by many people today, in their struggle to reduce – often at the same time – carbohydrates, chloresterol, proteins, calories, and alcohol.

Children were supposed to be born phlegmatic. Luckily, they were given foods which were not only right according to the Tudors' rules, but were of real dietary value – milk and dairy produce, for example. As

Left Conversation with a doctor

Consultation of two doctors

Left Amputating a man's leg:
there were no real anaesthetics
in Tudor times

the years passed, children were supposed to grow more sanguine or
choleric, and adjusted their diet accordingly. In many households who
could afford it, babes-in-arms were given to wet nurses for breast
feeding; it was considered important to choose the nurse not only for
her milk-giving abilities, but also for her moral qualities – since the
child was supposed to imbibe these along with the milk.

Old folk were thought to revert to the phlegmatic state of infancy as
they grew older, and of course were supposed to go back to a child's diet.

The Tudor period did witness some important advances in medical
knowledge. Leonardo da Vinci had pioneered anatomical drawing,
and Andreas Vesalius of Padua produced his famous textbook on
anatomy in 1543. The first man to relate anatomy to surgery was a
Frenchman, Ambroise Paré (1510–90), "the greatest surgeon of the
Renaissance," who ended the agonies of red-hot cauteries after amputa-
tions by the use of a simple ligature. Paré also pioneered the use of
artificial limbs, with which he experimented on wounded soldiers. He
treated gunshot wounds with a soothing salve instead of boiling oil, as
earlier practice had dictated, in the belief that gun shot was poisonous.
Three great surgeons practised the new work in England – Thomas
Gale, William Clowse, and John Woodall. Yet the Tudors in general
were suspicious of continental surgery and pharmacy, and slow to adopt
them into native practice.

Doctors

There were precious few physicians and surgeons in Tudor England.
Those that were there lived for the most part in the dozen or so largest
cities, including London, and made their living by attending the nobility
and rich merchant families. These doctors often had a degree from the
university of Oxford, or perhaps from Padua in Italy, which was a
centre of medical study at that time. A doctor who settled in a provincial
town might establish his practice by taking on an apprentice, just like
any merchant or craftsman. The normal fee for a doctor's visit at
that time was one mark, or about 67p; considering that a farmworker
might only earn a few coppers a week, this was a substantial sum of
money.

It is interesting to see how different people went about securing

Left A doctor at a sick bed

medical help. The borough of Denbigh, for example, actually elected a surgeon as a burgess, in return for his help "at all times to heale and cure every burgess dwelling in the said town . . . taking such wages for every the said cures as the Aldermen, Bayliffes, and Capitall Burgesses . . . shall award." This amounted to a kind of private patients' club.

England did have more than a hundred hospitals in the Tudor period – mostly small convalescent dwellings attached to monasteries or convents, where monks or nuns provided nursing care as a charitable act. But when Henry VIII closed down the monasteries after his break with the Pope in the 1530s, virtually all these hospitals disappeared. The loss of the hospitals, inadequate as they may have been, caused a public outcry, and Henry VIII refounded two of the London hospitals soon afterwards – St. Bartholomew's in 1544, and Bethlehem Hospital for lunatics in 1547, the last year of his reign. Edward VI refounded St. Thomas's in 1552, and the disused royal palace of Bridewell, formerly used as a house of correction for vagrants, became one of the royal hospitals in 1557. Some provincial hospitals, were reopened too, for example at Winchester and York but the shortage of hospitals was still acute.

Alcoholic fumes being used for anaesthesia

Of course, a king or queen would demand greater personal attention. For example, Queen Elizabeth once contracted a toothache while staying at Kenilworth. She was understandably frightened, since even a toothache could prove fatal, if the abcess infected the rest of the body. Her doctors could do nothing to relieve the pain, and the matter was put before the Privy Council. At length, a doctor called John Anthony Fenatus was summoned, though many felt it was "very risky to entrust the Queen's tooth to a foreigner who might be a Jew or a Papist." But Elizabeth flatly refused to have the tooth drawn. At this, Thomas Aylmer, the Bishop of London, volunteered to have a tooth drawn in her presence, so that she would see that the pain of the extraction was not too unbearable. The extraction was duly performed on the Bishop, and Elizabeth consented to have her own tooth drawn – to the relief not only of herself but the Privy Council and everyone else besides.

Folk medicine

Humbler folk relied almost entirely on superstition and folk medicine

Above Operating on a man's ear:
operations were dangerous
because not much was known
about infection

Right A sixteenth-century dentist

Below A herb garden: herbs
were very useful both in
medicine and cooking

for their cures. Some of these were extraordinary: a victim of falling
sickness might be cured by drinking spring water at night from the
skull of someone who had been slain; a woman could be released from
travail if someone threw a stone over the house where she lay – but only
if the stone was one which had killed three living creatures, a man, a wild
boar and a she bear (such stones must have been hard to come-by,
except at the hands of quacks and pedlars). The ague, or fever, might
be cured by cutting an apple into three pieces, and writing on them,
"The Father is Uncreated," "The Father is Incomprehensible", and
"The Father is Eternal."

In the sixteenth century herbs were very widely grown for their
medicinal properties, and many new species were imported from the
continent, especially from Italy. One doctor Bombastus, a Swiss–German
who preferred the name Paracelsus, devised a whole new science: the
"doctrine of signatures." He believed that every plant was "signed" –
associated by shape, colour or odour – with a specific disease. The plant
was therefore the "specific" with which the disease was treated. Lung-
wort, for example, was used for lung ailments, since the plant vaguely
resembled the lungs in shape. (The suffix *wort* had for centuries indicated
plants with medicinal properties). Bombastus's theories remained in
vogue for many years after his death, and were widely practised by
physicians, apothecaries, herbalists and astrologers, no doubt in com-
bination – in typical Tudor fashion – with the sciences of the stars,
and the humours of the body.

Left An operation on the skull
Above Tudor cartoon on the
treatment of the sick

Robert Burton wrote that, "Many an old wife or country woman doth often more good with a few known and common garden herbs than our bombast physicians with all their prodigious, sumptuous, far-fetched rare conjectural medicine." A headache might be cured if the sufferer drank a mixture of aniseed, betony, calamint, eyebright, lavender, bay, roses, rue, sage, marjoram and foal's foot; a sufferer of poor lungs a "comfrey" of calamint, liquorice, campanula and hyssop. He should also avoid sour or tart foods, and eat or drink cordials and restoratives.

Those who complained of bad hearts would use borage, bugloss, saffron, balm, basil, rosemary and roses; stomach sufferers would use wormwood, mint, betony, balm, centaury, sorrel and purslane. They had especially to avoid all foods which "engender wind" such as peas, beans and pottage.

The Breviary of Health

Books on health were fairly widely printed and distributed in Tudor times. One of the best known was Andrew Borde's *Breviary of Health*. This contained, for example, some rather curious detailed rules for the preservation of good eyesight. "Everything that is green or black is good for a man to look upon it. Also to look upon gold is good for the sight, and so is glass, cold water, and everything cold, except the wind, is good for the eyes, and no hot thing, nor warm thing, is good for the eyes except woman's milk and the blood of a dove. These things be evil for the eye: everything that is hot is not for the eyes, the sun, the fire, the snow and everything that is white is not good for the sight, and smoke, weeping, the wind, sickness, rheume, reading in small printed books, specially Greek books, and onions, garlic, chibols and suchlike be not good for the eyes. To clarify the eyes and the sight, take the seeds of *oculi christi* and put into eyes two, three or four seeds, or else take cold water and with a fine linen cloth wash the eyes divers times in a day, the oftener the better, and change the water often that it may be fresh and cold."

Borde also had something to say about deafness. According to him, this might overtake someone in three ways – through nature, accident, or a humour which blocks the hearing organs. His remedy was as follows: "If it come by nature, that is to say that one is born deaf, there is no manner of remedy but only God to do a miracle. If it do come accidentally, as by a stroke, a stripe, a bruise, or a fall or suchlike, and that by it the organs of hearing be closed up, there is no remedy but only God. If it do come of an humour, there is remedy as thus: First put nothing into the ear except it be warm as blood. Then take the gall of a hare and mix it with the grease of a fox and with black wool instil it into the ear. Or else take of the juice of wormwood and temper it with the gall of a bull and intinct [soak] black wool in it; put into the ear."

Borde had remedies for nearly every bodily complaint, including baldness: "Shave the head and beard, and anoint the head with the grease of a fox. Or else wash the head with the juice of beets five or six times, or else stamp garlic and rub the head with it and after wash it

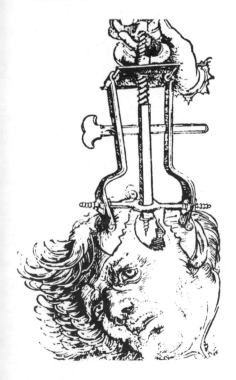

A patient enduring the pain of an operation on the skull with no anaesthetic

Above A surgical operation in the sixteenth century.
Below left A surgeon cauterising a wound with a hot iron.
Right An amputation: the patient is blindfolded and the priest reads prayers to him

with vinegar. Do this five or six times. Or else make ashes of garlic and temper it with honey and anoint the head . . . Anoint the head with the oils of bitter almonds, or with the oil of wormwood, or with the oil of spycarnad and suchlike oils. . . . The oil of myrtles is good, or the oil of galls, or the oil of walnuts or the oil of maidenhair."

Borde also offered a cure for sleeplessness. This was, incidentally, caused by "idleness or weakness of the brain, or else through sickness, anger or fasting, or else through solicitude or repletion, or extreme heat or extreme cold in the feet or such like." His remedy was to "take of the oil of violets an ounce, of opium half an ounce, incorporate this together with woman's milk and with a fine linen cloth lay it to the temples, or else use to eat of lettuce seeds, of white poppy seeds, or mandragor seeds . . . of each three drams, but above all things mirth is best to bed-ward."

Plague

The rat catcher destroyed rats with the help of his cat and the bag of poisons at his belt

One of the curses of Tudor England was smallpox, against which there was no prevention, and for which there was no real cure. Queen Elizabeth herself, along with thousands of her subjects, bore the heavy scars of smallpox which no amount of cosmetics could fully conceal in those lucky enough to survive the disease. It was customary, when someone contracted smallpox, to cover the windows of the sick room with red cloth, such as a red petticoat. This had been the practice since the reign of Edward I. Curiously enough, modern scientists have found that many kinds of red material or red objects have the effect of filtering out the deadly actinic sun rays which cause the scarring.

Much of the reason for disease was that the Tudors had little sense of hygiene. The common people seldom bathed; baths were hardly known in the houses of the rich; pestilence struck often and terribly, especially cholera and smallpox. Burials were sometimes perfunctorily performed, and the corpses of criminals were frequently left hanging on public gallows, and the heads of the executed left on the pikes on London Bridge (as an example to others). Filth and slops were thrown out into the streets; there was no sewage system, no refuse disposal apart from what the elements and the weather provided. Rats and other pests infested the towns.

Yet, if there was a danger of pestilence, it was not easy for a man to decide to leave his home for the cleaner air of the countryside. As this conversation from *A Dialogue Against the Pestilence* (1564) by William Bullein shows:

Citizen. "Good wife, the daily jangling and ringing of the bells, the coming in of the Minister to every house in ministring the communion, in reading the homily of death, the digging up of graves, the sparring in of windows, and the blazing forth of the blue cross, do make my heart tremble and quake. Alas, what shall I do to save my life?"

Wife. "Sir, we are but young, and have but a time in this world, what doth it profit us to gather riches together, and can not enjoy them? Why tarry we here so long? I do think every hour a year until we be gone . . . seeing that we have sent our children forth three weeks past into a good air and a sweet country, let us follow them. . . . Let us take leave of our neighbours, and return merely home again when the plague is past, and the dog days ended."

Madness

As one might expect, insanity was not understood in any modern sense. To most people madmen were freaks. Andrew Borde believed there were four kinds of madness – mania, melancholia, frenisis, and demoniacus. Maniacs in their madness "be full of divination, as thinking themselves to conjure or to create or to make things that no man can do but God, and doth presume upon supernatural things, thinking that they can think or do the things which it is impossible for man to do.

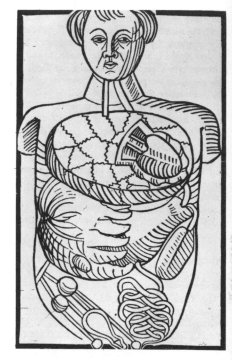

An anatomical drawing of a man: medicine became a little more scientific during the sixteenth century

"Melancholia is another kind of madness, and they the which are infested with this madness be ever in fear and dread, and doth things that they shall never do well, but ever be in peril from either of soul or body or both, wherefore thy do flee from one place to another, and cannot tell where to be except they be kept in safeguard.

"Frenisis is another kind of madness, and it doth come ever in a fever. They do rave and speak, and cannot tell what they say.

"Demoniacus is another kind of madness, and they who are in this madness be ever possessed of the devil, and be devilish persons, and will do much harm and evil, worse than they which be maniacs, for maniac persons comes of infirmities of the body, but demoniac persons be possessed of some evil spirit." Those unfortunates who suffered from epilepsy or similar fevers had little to hope from their Tudor contemporaries, especially if they were locked away in Bedlam (Bethlehem Hospital, London, for lunatics).

In his *Compendyous Regiment* (1567) Borde advocated stern treatment of lunatics: "It appared of late days of a lunatick man named Michel, the which went many years at liberty, and at last he did kyll his wife and his wife's sister, and his own self, wherefore I do advertyse everyman the which is mad . . . to be kept in safeguard, in some close house or chamber, where there is lyttle light. And that he have a keeper the whiche the madde man do feare. . . . Also the chamber . . . that the madde man is in, let there be no paynted clothes, nor paynted walls, nor pyctures. . . . For such things maketh them full of fantasyes. . . . And use fewe words to them, except it be for reprehension, or gentyll reformacion if they have any witte to understand."

Indeed, the Tudor period was not one which held out much hope to those who were sick either in mind or in body.

Above Boys playing a variety of different games

Below Children's games in the sixteenth century

6 *Learning and the Arts*

SELDOM in English history has education been placed at a higher premium than in the Tudor period – a period which saw a great revival of learning, and the foundation of many new grammar schools.

Hugh Rhodes explained in his *Book of Nurture* (1577), "There is fewe thinges to be understand more necessary then to teache and governe Children in learning and good manners, for it is a hye servyce to God, it getteth favour in the syghte of men, it multiplyeth goods, and increaseth thy good name. It also provoketh to prayer by whiche God's grace is obtayned, if thus they bee brought up in vertue, good maners, and Godly learning.

"The cause of the world being so evill of lyving as it is, is for lack of vertue, and Godly bringing up of youth. Whych youth sheweth the disposytions and conditions of their Parentes or Maysters, under whome they have bene governed. For youth is disposed to take such as they are accustomed in, good or evill. For if the behavyour of the governour be evill, needes must the Chylde be evill."

Education for gentlemen

Rhodes suggested that fathers and mothers should encourage their children to use "fayre and gentle speeche" and reverence and courtesy towards their elders and betters, "rebuking as well their ydle talke and stammering, as their uncomely jestures in going or standing."

As to schooling, Rhodes advised the parents to see that their masters feared God, and lived virtuously. They should punish sharply with patience and not with rigour, "for it doth oft times make them to rebell and run away, whereof chaunceth oft tymes much harme."

It was the parents' duty to instruct their children in God's laws, so that "litle by litle they shall come to the knowledge of reason, fayth and good Christen living."

> *When that thou comest to the Church, thy prayers for*
> *to say,*
> *See thou sleepe not, nor yet talke not, devoutly*
> *looke thou pray,*
> *Ne cast thyne eyes to ne fro, as thinges thou*
> *wouldst still see;*
> *So shall wyse men judge thee a foole, and wanton*
> *for to bee.*
> *When thou are in the Temple, see thou do thy Churchly*
> *warkes;*
> *Heare thou Gods word with diligence, crave pardon*
> *for thy fautes.*

F

Christ's Hospital where boys and girls from poor homes were given
a good education

For a boy of noble birth, education did not simply mean learning
grammar, theology and the classics at grammar school – it meant
preparing in every way for his station in life as a courtier, soldier and
landowner. A tutor wrote this report on one of his pupils whose father
was the Earl of Essex, Secretary to King Henry VIII: "He exerciseth
his hand in writing one or two hours, and readeth upon Fabian's
Chronicle as long. The residue of the day he doth spend upon the lute
and virginals. When he rideth, as he doth very oft, I tell him by the way
some history of the Romans or Greeks, which I cause him to rehearse
again in a tale. For his recreation he useth to hawk and hunt, and shoot
in his longbow, which frameth and succeedeth so well with him that
he seemeth to be thereunto given by Nature."

The greatest educationalist of Tudor times was Roger Ascham. In his
book *The Schoolmaster* (1570) he wrote: "to ride comely, to run fair at
the tilt or ring, to play at all weapons, to shoot fair in bow or surely in
gun, to vault lustily, to run, to leap, to wrestle, to swim; to dance comely
to sing and play of instruments cunningly, to hawk, to hunt, to play at
tennis and at all pastimes generally, which be joined with labour, used
in open place and in the daylight, containing either some fit exercise
for war, or some pleasant pastime for peace, be not only comely and
decent, but also very necessary for a courtly gentleman to use."

Schools

The Tudor period saw education at all levels in a flourishing state; and even today the English still benefit from the Tudor legacy in this field. All kinds of schools existed, and it was usually possible for an intelligent boy, and even a girl if she was lucky, to receive some kind of education at almost any level of society. Before Henry VIII dissolved the monasteries there were many schools run by the monks, principally for the training of novices. Many cathedrals and churches had their own choir school, where boys could receive an education during the time not spent singing in church services. Most of the large towns had their own grammar schools, locally endowed for the sons of merchants and guildsmen. Eton had been founded in 1440 for "twentyfive poor and needy scholars to learn grammar there." Many local churches had chantry schools attached to them, where the priest would give lessons to local children as part of the terms of the church's endowment. These were some of the best known grammar schools founded in the Tudor period; all of them survive today:

Part of a writing master's copy sheet

1509 St. Paul's
1541 Berkhamstead
1550 Sherbourne
1551 Shrewsbury
1552 Bedford
1557 Repton
1565 Highgate
1567 Rugby
1571 Harrow
1584 Uppingham

In his *Travels in England* (1599) Thomas Platter gives an interesting example of an early coeducational school, Christ's Hospital. It was "founded by a great lady, and already in progress during her lifetime, which hospital finds food and drink and clothes for seven hundred

Far left A book-plate from one of the early grammar schools (St. Albans). *Left* Book-plate of Sir Nicholas Bacon

A schoolroom where several lessons are taking place

young boys and girls, while reading and writing are taught in special schools in the same, and they are kept there until they are fit for some craft or service, when they are taken away and put out wherever they like, or opportunity offers, boys and girls alike. They are all fine children, taken from poor parents and put in here. They keep their hospital exceedingly clean – in the boys' long apartment are one hundred and forty beds in a row on either side, where they sleep two and two together, and by their beds they have low chests in which to keep their clothes. There are fewer girls in a smaller room."

Boys usually first learned their "letters" – reading and writing – at home, or sometimes at the hands of a local priest, or at a "petty school" – a preparatory school attached to one of the great grammar schools. In the families of the gentry, it was often the practice to send the sons away to stay with friends, where a group of the boys could be privately tutored together in small classes. The teaching in these classes was often of a more modern kind than was found in the formal grammar schools and colleges. For example, the students might learn a foreign language such as French or Latin, or perhaps Welsh. As the dramatist Ben Jonson put it,

> *Where can he learn to vault, to ride, to fence,*
> *To move his body gracefuller, to speak*
> *His language purer, or to tune his mind*
> *Or manners more to the harmony of Nature*
> *Than in these nurseries of nobility?*

The sons of poorer families, who aspired to learn reading and writing, and perhaps to draw up accounts, found education a harder business.

A Tudor theatre: it is octagonal in shape and the roof is open to the sky

Parsons whose stipend was £100 or more were supposed to pay to send a promising student to university. But few parsons earned this sum and the education was more often dispensed by bellringers, sextons, or "poor women or others whose necessities compel them to undertake it as a mere shelter from beggary." In Tudor times, the state accepted no responsibility for providing education. It merely sought to encourage its provision by priests and others qualified.

Latin was the subject mainly taught in Tudor schools, as in Oxford and Cambridge. A large part of the child's day was taken up with learning Latin grammar and sentence construction. Printers produced books of grammar, some of which were early best-sellers. One of these was called *Vulgaria*, by William Horman, published quite early in 1519. These were some of the sentences to be translated into Latin:

> Whereas a flint or another stone to smite fire cannot be got, it must be done with rubbing of two treen (i.e. wooden) pieces together.
> I shall get me dry toadstools or fine linnen cloth, half burnt, to make tinder of.
> Lay this flesh in the brine lest it be lost (i.e. spoiled).
> Peel some cloves of garlic and stamp them.
> Wash all the greasy dishes and vessel in the lead cauldron or pan in hot water, and set them clean upon the scullery board.
> Take a wisp of straw and ashes and scour this pot.
> Set the earthen pot by him self for (i.e. to prevent) breaking.
> These rags will serve for kitchen cloths.

The Tudors were not averse to making the solemn business of education amusing as well. Here, for example, are two early educational toys devised by Sir Hugh Platt to encourage children to learn their alphabet and grammar. He wrote, "Cause four large dice of bone or wood to be made, and upon every square one of the small letters [of the alphabet] to be graven, but in some bigger shape. . . . The child using to play much with them, and being always told what letter chanceth, will soon gain his Alphabet, as it were by the way of sport or pastime. I have heard of a pair of cards, whereon most of the principall Grammar rules have been printed, and the School-Master hath found good sport thereat with his schollers."

There was no teacher-training in the Tudor period, and those who endowed schools, or who were responsible for organizing private tuition, simply had to find the best people they could – a priest perhaps, or even an intelligent servant good with children. This poem is a satire on the problem of finding good teachers. It appeared in Joseph Hall's *Satires* of 1597:

A gentle squire would gladly entertain
*Into his house some trencher-chappelain;** *
Some willing man that might instruct his sons,
And that would stand to good conditions.
First, that he lie upon the truckle-bed,
Whiles his young master lieth o'er his head.
Second, that he do, on no default,
Ever presume to sit above the salt.
Third, that he never change his trencher twice.
Fourth, that he use all common courtesies;
Sit bare at meals, and one half rise and wait.
Last, that he never his young master beat,
But he must ask his mother to define,
How many jerks she would his breech should line,
All these observed, he could contented be,
To give five marks and winter livery.

* A priest fond of good dinners.

Top and above French cards for a game of piquet

Right The interior King Edward VI's Grammar School at Stratford-on-Avon

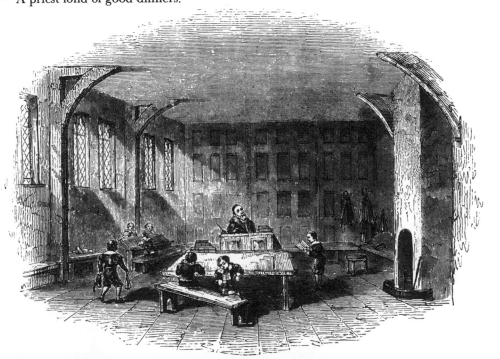

The Universities

William Harrison described England's universities in his *Description of England* (1587). "In my time there are three noble universities in England, to wit, one at Oxford, the second at Cambridge, and the third in London, of which the first two are the most famous." The subjects taught included languages, philosophy and the "liberal sciences", and "the profound studies of the civil law, physic and theology," but the students at London learned only law. Oxford and Cambridge had the great benefit of generations of generous endowments, endowments which were continued in the Tudor age. This had enabled them to acquire "divers goodly brick houses builded four square . . . of hard freestone or brick" – most buildings at that time were of wood – "with great numbers of lodgings and chambers in the same for students, after a sumptuous manner, through the exceeding liberality of kings, queens, bishops, noblemen and ladies of the land; but also large livings and great revenues bestowed upon them the like whereof is not seen in any other region. . . ."

In the colleges of Oxford and Cambridge, the students were amply provided for, and so were not forced into common lodging houses and taverns like their counterparts on the continent. "In these our colleges we live in such order [as] exceeded all the monastical institutions that ever were devised." Altogether, Harrison estimated that there were three thousand students at Oxford and Cambridge, a far higher proportion of the population even than today.

It was not easy to get into Oxford or Cambridge, as William Harrison explained: "They were erected by their founders at the first, only for poor men's sons, whose parents were not able to bring them up unto learning. But now they have the least benefit of them, by reason the rich do so encroach upon them. And so far hath this inconvenience spread itself that it is in my time an hard matter for a poor man's child to come by a fellowship, though he be never so good a scholar and worthy of that room." The unworthy students "ruffle and roist it out, exceeding in apparel and haunting riotous company which draweth them from their books." Harrison added that the elections were so rigged that the places went to "he who hath most friends . . . is always surest to speed, which will turn in the end to the overthrow of learning." His words indeed were to prove true enough; by the eighteenth century both Oxford and Cambridge had reached an all-time low in scholastic standing.

In his *Travels in England* (1598), Paul Henztner found that Oxford and Cambridge students led a monastic life, devoted almost entirely to their studies. The university body was divided into three "tables" – "The first is called the Fellows' table, to which are admitted earls, barons, gentlemen, doctors and masters of arts, but very few of the latter. This is more plentifully and expensively served than the other." The second table was for masters of arts, bachelors, a few gentlemen and eminent citizens. The third table was for people "of low condition." During dinner in the great hall of a college, each student in turn would be appointed to read aloud from the Bible. After grace had been said at the end of the meal, everyone was free to retire to his chambers or walk in the delightful college gardens. The students' dress was almost the

same as that of the Jesuits, "their gowns reaching down to their ankles, sometimes lined with fur. They wear square caps. Doctors, masters of arts and professors have another kind of gown that distinguishes them." Every student of standing had his own key to the heart of the college's treasures, the library.

In the late 1500s, a good room at Oxford University cost from 50p to £1 a year, although the cost could be reduced if students shared one another's lodgings. The students had to provide all their own furniture, linen and table ware, and fuel. In all, a young gentleman of means might spend £20 a year as a fulltime student. Some students ate in their lodgings, or in local taverns, for a few shillings or a few pence. Others dined at the college table, often on "boiled beef with pottage, bread and beer, and no more." Despite the chancellors' rules banning extravagant dress, and idling in taverns, there was a great difference to be seen between the wealthy students and the poor ones.

The curriculum at both school and university was based on the system of the old Roman Empire – the *trivium* (Latin grammar, logic, rhetoric)

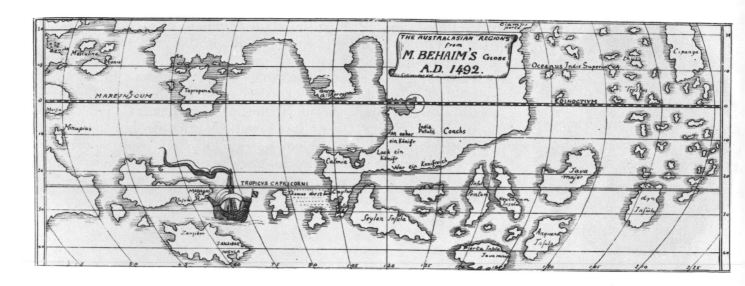

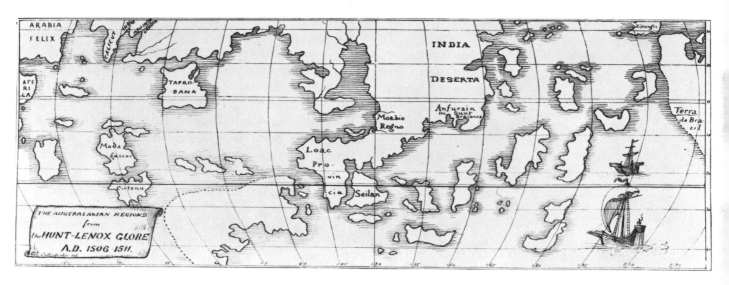

and the *quadrivium* (arithmetic, geometry, astronomy, and music). Greek was a relatively new study, and was not yet universally accepted. Students could now read many printed books, something made possible by the invention of the moveable type printing presses of Johann Gutenberg and others, and used in England by printers like William Caxton. They could buy grammars, Bibles, books of Arabic, algebra and arithmetic, books on husbandry and zoology, and astronomy – though the new discoveries of Copernicus were not yet assimilated, and the telescope still lay in the future. Many of these books were written by prominent teachers of the time, such as the historian and topographer William Camden (1551–1623), who was headmaster of Westminster School in London. Hakluyt's *Voyages* was eagerly read by students of geography. Writing was almost a specialist art, often taught by expert "scriveners" who travelled from one school to another. English, as a language and body of literature, was barely taught at all, except through the medium of Latin, which was still then a living language.

Students at both school and university were tested in two ways – in the

Top The Australasian Regions on Martin Behaim's Globe: the Tudor period was a great age of discovery. *Above* The Australasian Regions on the Hunt–Lenox Globe *Below* Westminster School in London

Francis Bacon

written theme, and the oral disputation, or debate, all of which were done in Latin. Often the debates ended in riotous disorder, with the angry students falling to "blows with their satchels full of books." The student's apprenticeship was a long one: four years to achieve the status of bachelor of arts, and a further three years to become a "master". Vacations were much shorter than they are now: twelve days at Christmas and twelve days at Easter, with certain other holidays as well.

The results of the educational system, such as it was, available in Elizabethan times, were good. Literacy may well have been higher, nationally, then than it was in the dark days of the industrial revolution of the nineteenth century.

Value of travel

"Travel in the younger sort," said Francis Bacon, "is a part of education." The Elizabethan essayist told the young traveller abroad to travel with a good tutor as companion, and to make an accurate record of all the wonders that he saw. Few people in the sixteenth century had the opportunity for travel: most travellers were officials on some royal or church business, priests, clerks, lawyers, secretaries, diplomats, merchants. A young gentleman in his late teens might well occupy such a post in adulthood, and extended travel abroad might both widen his horizons and equip him for later work. Bacon advised, "Let him carry with him also some card or book describing the country where he travelleth, which will be a good key to his enquiry. Let him also keep a diary."

It would be a mistake to stay too long in one city or town. Indeed, "When he stayeth in one city or town let him change his lodging from one end and part of the town to another. . . . Let him sequester himself from the company of his countrymen, and diet in such places where there is good company of the nation. . . . Thus he may abridge his travel with much profit." And on his return home, the younger traveller should maintain a lively correspondence with his newfound friends abroad. He should, incidentally, not forget his English manners in taking up continental customs.

Journey–Ring or *Viatorium* of 1587, an early navigational aid

Every Englishman who travelled abroad for pleasure tried to visit Italy, the home of the great renaissance in the arts and sciences. Indeed, the Italian influence became very strong in English social life – costume, food and drink, houses and gardens, music and literature. In *The Schoolmaster* (1570) Roger Ascham deplored this trend, remarking that although Italy was once the greatest nation of the earth, "That time is gone, and though the place remain, yet the old and present manners do differ as far as black and white, as virtue and vice." Ascham spoke of evil vices and corruption – "the enchantments of Circe" – which the young travellers brought back with them to England, and deplored the new flood of cheap Italian books which promoted "papistry".

Printing

A sign of the reawakening of intellectual life in England was the growing

THE PRINCIPALL
NAVIGATIONS, VOIA-
GES AND DISCOVERIES OF THE
English nation, made by Sea or ouer Land,
to the most remote and farthest distant Quarters of
the earth at any time within the compasse
of these 1500. yeeres: Deuided into three
seuerall parts, according to the po-
sitions of the Regions wherun-
to they were directed.

The first, conteining the personall trauels of the English vnto *Iud&a, Syria, A-*
rabia, the riuer *Euphrates, Babylon, Balsara,* the Persian Gulfe, *Ormuz, Chaul,*
Goa, India, and many Islands adioyning to the South parts of *Asia:* together with the like vnto *Egypt,* the chiefest ports and places of *Africa* within and without the Streight of *Gibraltar,* and about the famous Promon-
torie of *Buona Esperanza.*

The second, comprehending the worthy discoueries of the English towards
the North and Northeast by Sea, as of *Lapland, Scriksinia, Corelia,* the Baie
of *S. Nicholas,* the Isles of *Colgoieue, Vaigats,* and *Noua Zembla* toward the
great riuer *Ob,* with the mightie Empire of *Russia,* the *Caspian Sea, Georgia,*
Armenia, Media, Persia, Boghar in *Bactria,* & diuers kingdoms of *Tartaria.*

The third and last, including the English valiant attempts in searching almost all the corners of the vaste and new world of *America,* from 73. de-
grees of Northerly latitude Southward, to *Meta Incognita, Newfoundland,*
the maine of *Virginia,* the point of *Florida,* the Baie of *Mexico,* all the In-
land of *Noua Hispania,* the coast of *Terra firma, Brasill,* the riuer of *Plate,* to
the Streight of *Magellan:* and through it, and from it in the South Sea to
Chili, Peru, Xalisco, the Gulfe of *California, Noua Albion* vpon the backside
of *Canada,* further then euer any Christian hitherto hath pierced.

Whereunto is added the last most renowmed English Nauigation,
round about the whole Globe of the Earth.

By Richard Hakluyt Master of Artes, and Student sometime
of Christ-church in Oxford.

Imprinted at London by GEORGE BISHOP
and RALPH NEWBERIE, Deputies to
CHRISTOPHER BARKER, Printer to the
Queenes most excellent Maiestie.

1589.

THE
SEAMANS SE-
CRETS.

Deuided into 2. partes, wherein is taught the
three kindes of Sayling, Horizontall, Paradoxall, and sayling vpon
a great Circle : also an Horizontall Tyde Table for the easie finding
of the ebbing and flowing of the Tydes, with a Regiment newly calcu-
lated for the finding of the Declination of the Sunne, and many other most necessary rules and Instruments, not
heeretofore set foorth by any.

Newly published by *Iohn Dauis* of *Sandrudge,* neere
Dartmouth, in the County of *Deuon.* Gent.

¶ *Imprinted at London by* Thomas Dawson,
dwelling at the three Cranes in the Vinetree,
and are these to be solde. 1595.

Above left The title page of a sixteenth-century book about
navigation and voyages of discovery.
Right A sixteenth-century guide to seamanship
Below Sixteenth-century pilgrims

THE FAERIE
QVEENE.

Diſpoſed into twelue books,
Fashioning
XII. Morall vertues.

LONDON
Printed for William Ponſonbie.
1 5 9 0.

The Faerie Queene by Edmund
Spenser (1590)

Above William Tyndale who translated the Bible into English.
Below Archbishop Cranmer presenting the Great Bible in English
to Henry VIII

Left A Tudor paper mill. Wet rag
is pulped by the mill, formed
into sheets and finished in the
wooden press

demand for books. Already William Caxton (1422–91) had set up his
printing press in London, and established himself as a publisher,
translator and bookseller. He produced his books both in Latin – where
they were of wide European interest – and increasingly in English. Here
there was both a difficulty and a challenge, for in the absence of diction-
aries and other printed matter, the English style and spelling was in a
state of change. Each part of the country had its own dialects, which
would often be hardly understood by other Englishmen living only a
hundred miles away.

Through the increasing output of his press, Caxton was able to make a
major contribution towards unifying the English language. He did this
after 1476, when he returned home after an absence of many years in
Europe. There are few industries in English history which can have

owed so much to the achievement of a single man. Of the 90-odd books produced by Caxton, no less than 74 were in English as opposed to Latin. He produced not only grammars and other reference works, but also popular works of entertainment such as *Aesop's Fables* and Geoffrey Chaucer's *The Canterbury Tales*. After Caxton's death in 1491, his work was carried on by his famous assistant, Wynkyn de Worde, a native of Alsace. Wynkyn's own output by the time of his own death in 1535 amounted to no less than 800 titles, some two-fifths of them intended for use by boys in grammar schools. Although Henry VIII violently opposed the translation of the Scriptures into English for most of his reign – necessitating printing in Paris and elsewhere abroad – he did finally accept an English translation of the Bible, known as the Great Bible, in 1539. Seven editions then followed within the next two years.

The editions printed by William Caxton, Richard Pynson, Richard Grafton and other leading printers were small compared with modern standards. On their cumbrous wooden printing presses, they produced only perhaps two hundred copies of each title. But one should remember that this was nevertheless a vast improvement on the laborious work of the medieval scribe, who copied his manuscripts out one-by-one by hand. By Queen Elizabeth's accession the printing industry was well-established, even if it had to steer a delicate course amid the ever-changing religious policies handed down by the Tudor monarchs. The Stationers Company was duly incorporated by royal charter in 1557, and still exists today.

Above A portrait of William Shakespeare

Right Blackfriars Theatre, London

The theatre

Until the mid-sixteenth century virtually the only form of drama known to the English were the miracle and morality plays, in which local players enacted stories from the Bible. These were simple dramas of good and evil, often based on the life of a saint. However, one of the effects of the Reformation of the time of Henry VIII was to bring these into official disfavour, as being improper vehicles for sacred subjects.

Drama in its modern stage form really dates from the Elizabethan period. This has been described as "the crowning achievement of Elizabethan England in the field of literature. More so than any other literary creation the drama gathered up and expressed the emotional and intellectual life of the age in all its length, breadth, height and depth." (Prof. Black). Indeed, the stage virtually became a national cult. Stage drama took several forms. One of the most popular was the allegory or "dark conceit", in which the dramatist presented some contemporary issue, involving personalities of the time, in a thin disguise:

> *When Shakespeare, Jonson, Fletcher ruled the stage*
> *They took so bold a freedom with the age,*
> *That there was scarce a knave or fool in town*
> *Of any note, but had his picture shown.*

A ballad-monger singing from his ballad sheet

Below The Bear Garden Theatre which was on the south bank of the River Thames, beyond the jurisdiction of the City

A mystery play being performed in the open air

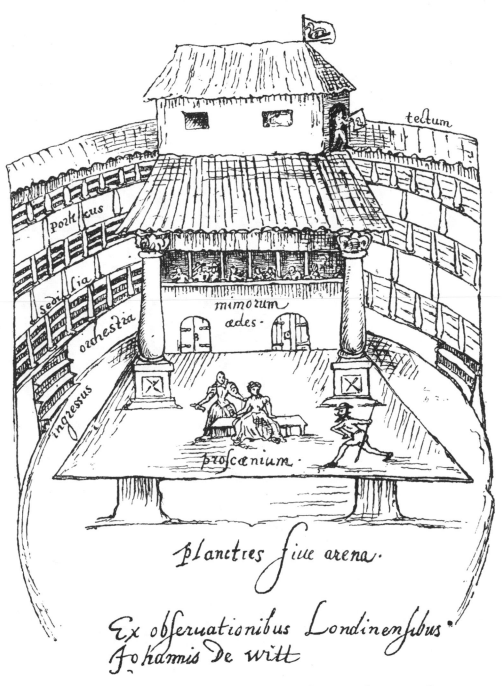

planeties siue arena.

Ex obseruationibus Londinensibus
Johannis De witt

Left The Swan Theatre London: the audience sat all around the stage

Of course, these performances delighted the crowds, eager for sensation, and many people of a Puritan disposition called upon the government to put a stop to all stage performances. Here, for example, is an extract from a petition by the Lord Mayor and Aldermen of London, calling upon the Privy Council in 1597 to ban stage plays:

"1. They are a special cause of corrupting their youth, containing nothing but unchaste matters, lascivious devices, shifts of cozenage, and other lewd and ungodly practices . . .

"2. They are the ordinary places for vagrant persons, masterless men, thieves, horse-stealers, whoremongers, cozeners, coney-catchers, contrivers of treason and other idle and dangerous persons to meet together and to make their matches to the great displeasure of Almighty God and the hurt and annoyance of her Majesty's people. This cannot be

Above The house in Stratford-upon-Avon in which Shakespeare was born

Below The house in Stratford where Shakespeare lived and died

prevented nor discovered by the governors of the city, for . . . they are out of the city's jurisdiction.

"3. They maintain idleness in such persons as have no vocation, and draw apprentices and other servants from their ordinary works . . . to the great hindrance of trades and profanation of religion established by her Highness within this realm.

"4. In the time of sickness it is found by experience that many, having sores and yet not heart-sick, take occasion hereby to walk abroad and to recreate themselves by hearing a play. Whereby others are infected, and themselves also many things miscarry."

In view of the hostility of the City of London, the acting profession found it necessary to put on their plays on the south side of the River Thames, where they were outside the city boundaries, and free from

Above The performance of one of Shakespeare's plays – "A Midsummer Nights Dream"

Right A play entitled *Arden at Feversham* based on a crime of the period

arrest. Here, the plays of Shakespeare and others drew large crowds.

As Thomas Platter wrote in 1599, "Daily at two in the afternoon, London has two, sometimes three plays running in different places, competing with each other, and those which play best obtain most spectators. The playhouses are so constructed that they play on a raised platform, so that everyone has a good view. There are different galleries and places, however, where the seating is better and more comfortable and therefore more expensive. For whoever cares to stand below only pays one English penny, but if he wishes to sit he enters by another door, and pays another penny, while if he desires to sit in the most comfortable seats which are cushioned, where he not only sees everything well, but can also be seen, then he pays yet another English penny at another door. And during the performance food and drink are carried round the audience, so that for what one cares to pay one may also have refreshment.

"The actors are most expensively and elaborately costumed; for it is the English usage for eminent lords or Knights at their decease to bequeath and leave almost the best of their clothes to their serving men, which it is unseemly for the latter to wear, so that they offer them for sale for a small sum to the actors. How much time then they may merrily spend daily at the play everyone knows who has ever seen them play or act."

The conditions for the audience were primitive. The plays had to be put on in daylight hours. There were no footlights, no stage curtain, and few scenic effects (though the costumes were much admired). Those who had friends in the theatre, or who could afford to pay, had stools on the stage among the actors. Everyone else had to stand in the pit below the stage or, if they were lucky, in the covered galleries encircling the stage. Stephen Gosson wrote in his *Schoole of Abuse* (1579): "In our assemblies at plays in London, you shall see such heaving, and shoving, such itching and shouldering to sit by women: such care for their garments, that they be not trod on: such eyes to their laps, that no chips light in

Below left The Globe Theatre, London. *Right* The Swan Theatre, London

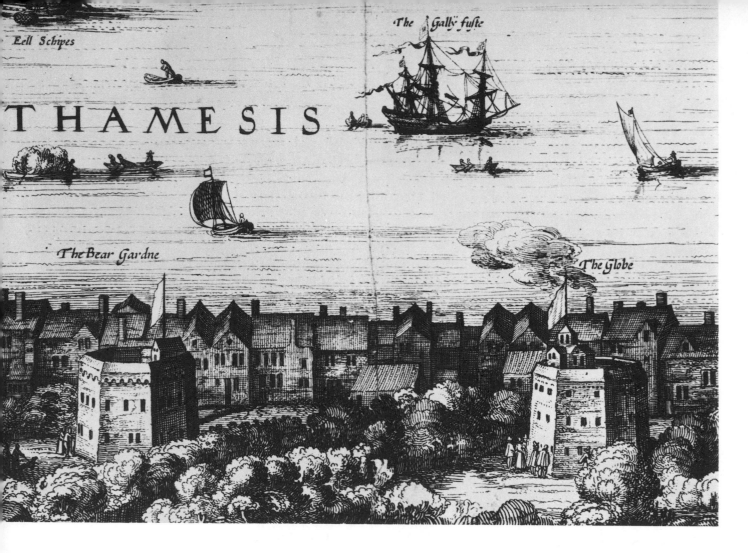

Eell Schipes

THAMESIS

The Gally fuste

The Bear Gardne

The Globe

The Globe Theatre and the Bear Garden, both on the south bank of the Thames

them: such pillows to their backs, that they take no hurt: such masking in their ears, I know not what: such giving them pippins to pass the time: such playing at foot-saunt without cards: such tickling, such toying, such smiling, such winking, and such manning them home, when the sports are ended, that it is a right comedy to mark their behaviour.''

As Gosson pointed out, one or two of the theatres would sink to almost any depths to attract customers if business was slack: "For they that lack customers all the week, either because their haunt is unknown or the constables and officers of their parish watch them so narrowly that they dare not quetch, to celebrate the sabbath flocks to theatres, and there keep a general market of bawdry. Not that any filthiness in deed is committed within the compass of that ground, as was done in Rome, but that every wanton and his paramour, every man and his mistress, every John and his Joan, every knave and his quean, are there first acquainted and cheapen the merchandise in that place, which they pay for elsewhere as they can agree.''

There were many travelling theatrical companies that went on tour to provincial cities. One writer remembered how as a boy he had been at Gloucester with his father when a theatrical company had arrived at the city. The local authorities exercised strong control over what entertainments were put on, and the company had first to seek the approval of the mayor and aldermen. If the mayor approved what was to be put on, a special public performance was staged in the city, in the presence of the mayor. The public had the chance of a free preview, at the mayor's expense, "the mayor giving the players a reward as he thinks fit to show respect to them."

R. Willis recalled, "At such a play my father took me with him, and made me stand between his legs as he sat upon one of the benches, where we saw and heard very well. The play was called *The Cradle of Security*, wherein was personated a king or some great prince." The play made a great impression on the young spectator. Writing many years later he said, "What great care should be had in the education of children, to keep them from seeing of spectacles of ill examples and hearing of lascivious or scurrilous words. . . . Their young memories are like fair writing tables."

Music

"Supper being ended, and musicke bookes (according to the custom) being brought to table, the mistress of the house presented me with a part, earnestly requesting me to sing. But when after many excuses I protested unfainedly that I could not, everyone began to wonder! Yes, some whispered to others, demanding how I was brought up, so that

Left Most well educated young ladies were musically accomplished

upon shame of mine ignorance I goe now to seek out mine old friend Master Gnorimus to make myself his scholar."

Such was the experience of one Englishman, who shamefacedly had to admit being tone-deaf. The Tudor period was a great age of music. As early as the reign of the music-loving Henry VIII, and even that of his father Henry VII, there existed a school of English music growing in distinction. It was represented particularly in Church music, the finest examples of which were performed at the Chapel Royal, embracing masses and motets by William Cornyshe, Robert Fairfax, Richard Sampson, John Tavener and other composers. Henry VII was a leading patron of music. The royal accounts show many purchases of flutes, clavichords, harps, and payments to choristers, pipers, harpers and other musicians. Henry VIII himself spent hundreds of pounds on lute-players, minstrels, virginal players, fifers and viol-players, and was careful to provide a musical education for his children Prince Edward, and the Princesses Mary and Elizabeth – all of them later to become monarchs.

Pleasure in musical accomplishment was shared by people from all walks and levels of life in Tudor England. Music supplied by village fiddlers and morris dancers was enjoyed in most parts of England whenever holidays or feast-days permitted. Sir Francis Drake even took an orchestra with him aboard the *Golden Hind* on his famous voyages. And there were few towns with any sense of civic pride which did not have their own resident band of singing "waits".

This great age of music and theatre testified to a changing English society. Under strong Tudor government, determined to foster national unity, the old warring feudal lords had gone, to be replaced by courtiers, and courtly patronage of the arts. This, together with the growing refinements in domestic life, and the changes in the pattern of life on the land, strengthens the claim of the Tudor period to be the great watershed between medieval and modern times.

Opposite: top left Dr. John Bull, Elizabeth I's organist. *Top right* A morris dancer wearing the traditional scarves and bells. *Centre right* An Elizabethan virginal: a popular keyboard instrument. *Below* Tudor musicians playing crumhorns and a clarion

Above A music party

The Tudor Cost of Living

It is difficult to make comparisons between prices and incomes in the Tudor period and the present day. But the following details will give some idea of Tudor income and prices in relation to one another. They are the actual amounts in Tudor money. 12 pence made 1 shilling, 20 shillings made £1 (or $2.50).

Income

Income of substantial merchant, £100 per annum upwards.

Income of country gentry, mostly £50 to £100 per annum, though some received £1,000 or more.

Annual wage of a maid, £4 downwards.

Income of a country parson, about £20 per annum.

Sir Walter Raleigh's income from his wine monopoly, £800 to £2,000 per annum.

English exports in the year 1564–65, £1,100,000.

The estate of the financier Sir Horatio Palavicino at his death in 1600 of £100,000 made him one of the handful of the richest men in England.

Wage of a Hertfordshire stonemason in 1592, on a scale ranging from eight to twelve pence a day.

Weekly wage of a carpenter in the reign of Queen Elizabeth, about five shillings.

Rough general average income of a Tudor peer, £1,000 per annum.

Income of Cardinal Wolsey in the 1520s, about £10,000 per annum, though this had risen to about £50,000 by the end of his life.

The Countess of Shrewsbury, Bess of Hardwicke, was second only to the Queen in personal wealth; her income was about £60,000 per annum according to one estimate.

Annual landed income of Lord Burghley, chief minister to Queen Elizabeth I, £4,000.

Annual income of Matthew Parker, Archbishop of Canterbury, £3,428.

Income of a stable-boy at Ingatestone Hall, ten shillings per quarter.

Income of the youngest maid at Ingatestone Hall, five shillings per quarter.

Income of the butler at Ingatestone Hall, ten shillings per quarter.

Income of a footman, about £2 to £6 a year.

Income of a watchman, about £1 to £2 per year.

Total aggregate value of a labourer's goods and chattels, about £10.

Total aggregate value of a craftsman's goods and chattels, about £20.

Wage of a labourer, threepence or fourpence a day.

Prices

Price of wheat in the early 1500s, five shillings or six shillings per quarter.
Price of wheat in the 1540s, about eleven shillings per quarter.
Price of wheat in the 1590s, about 35 shillings per quarter.
Cost of a 4-lb. loaf in the 1540s, 1½ pence.
Cost of a 4-lb. loaf in 1600, about 3d. or 4d.
A piece of fine russet broadcloth, about £6 for a 24-foot length.
Cost of a ton of Newcastle "sea coal", about £1 per ton.
Annual household expenses of the Earl of Derby in 1561, about £3,000.
Noblemen's dress: the Earl of Leicester once spent £563 on seven doublets and two cloaks.
Cost of the funeral of the Earl of Leicester, £3,000.
Cost of 12 pounds of candles, about three shillings.
Annual expenditure at Court of Queen Elizabeth I, £50,000.
A bottle of Gascony wine, two shillings.
A quail, a halfpenny.
Oysters (very good value in Tudor times), fourpence a bushel.
Price of 200 white herrings, three shillings,
A chicken, a penny.
Raisins, threepence a pound.
A goose, fourpence.
Best beef, about threepence a pound.
Best mutton, about 1½d a pound.
Sugar, about 4d a pound at the beginning of the Tudor period, more than a shilling at the end of it.
A two-pound jar of marmalade, about five shillings.
Cost of roofing tiles in 1500, about sixpence a 1,000.
Cost of building Kenilworth, the country seat of the Earl of Leicester, £60,000.
Cost of a stool furnished with red cloth, about 14 shillings.
Cost of a billiard table, £25 (purchased by the Earl of Bedford for his home at Woburn).
Canvas for use in making up servants' liveries, fourpence a yard.
Cost of a wedding gown in 1555 for the marriage of a knight's daughter, £11.
Cost of a student's Greek phrase book, about eightpence.
Cost of a dictionary, about ten shillings.
Cost of a table organ in the 1550s, £2.
Cost to the Earl of Leicester of entertaining Queen Elizabeth at Kenilworth Castle, estimated by a contemporary at £1,000 per day.
Cost of purchasing a farm cart, about £3.
Horseshoes, about twopence or threepence each, according to size.
Premium paid by an apprentice on entering the Goldsmith's Company, £10.
Premium paid by an apprentice on entering a lesser guild, £1 or £2.
Cost of cleansing the Fleet River in 1589, about £600.
A doctor's visit, 13s 4d. (66p).
Amount spent by Lord Burghley on maintaining his house at Theobalds Manor in Hertfordshire, up to £3,000 p.a.
Cost of a bedstead with a pair of blankets, for a knight, £1.

Cost of meals for a Cambridge student, about five shillings a week.

Cost of a meal at an Inn of Court, about threepence.

Student lodgings in the town, about two shillings a week including laundry.

Annual fees of Bedford Grammar School, including board, lodging and tuition, about £13.

A tankard of ale, about a halfpenny.

Charge made by Nicholas Hilliard for one of his miniatures, about £40.

Carriage charges from Oxford to London, 2s 4d (13p) per hundred-weight, or a halfpenny per pound for small items.

Carriage of letters, 1s 8d (8p) per stage. Queen Elizabeth spent about £5,000 per annum on letter deliveries.

Charge for post-horses, threepence a mile.

Cost of a pair of ornamental breeches, about £7 and upwards.

Cost of a pair of stockings, 15 shillings and upwards.

Cost of a fine shirt, about £1 and upwards.

Cost of a good pair of boots, about £4 to £10.

Annual budget of a student at Cambridge, about £20.

Coaching fees of a chorister, about £1 per annum.

Value of plate in a typical noble household, about £1,000 to £2,000.

A Tudor Time Chart

1485   The Battle of Bosworth. Henry Tudor becomes Henry VII and establishes the Tudor dynasty.

1492   Christopher Columbus discovers the New World.

1509   Death of Henry VII; accession of his son as Henry VIII.

1540   Probable year of birth of Francis Drake.

1542   Henry VIII makes witchcraft a capital offence.

1546   Death of Martin Luther, the Protestant reformer.

1547   Death of Henry VIII: accession of his son as Edward VI.

1552   Probable year of birth of Walter Raleigh, and the poet Edmund Spenser.

1553   Death of Edward VI; accession of his sister as Mary I. Start of the Catholic Counter-Reformation.

1558   Death of Mary I; Elizabeth I becomes Queen.

1563   { Statute of Artificers.
        { Act against Witchcraft.

1564   Birth of William Shakespeare.

1566   First witch trials at Chelmsford, Essex.

1572   Birth of the dramatist Ben Jonson.

1582   Marriage of William Shakespeare to Anne Hathaway.

1584   Reginald Scot publishes *The Discoverie of Witchcraft*.

1588   Defeat of the Spanish Armada.

1603   Death of Elizabeth; accession of James Stuart.

Further Reading

How They Lived (1585–1700), Molly Harrison and O. M. Royston (Blackwell, London, 1963; Barnes & Noble, New York, 1971)

Illustrated English Social History, Vol. 2, G. M. Trevelyan (Longmans, London, 1944; David McKay, New York, 1949)

A History of Everyday Things in England, Marjorie & C. H. B. Quennell (Batsford, London, 1919; Putnam, New York, 1956)

Elizabethan London, Martin Holmes (Cassell, London, 1969; Praeger, New York, 1971)

Tudor England, S. T. Bindoff, (Pelican, London, 1950; Penguin Books, Baltimore, 1950)

The Reign of Elizabeth, J. B. Black (Oxford University Press, 1959, Oxford University Press, New York, 1959)

The Earlier Tudors, J. D. Mackie (Oxford University Press, London, 1960; Oxford University Press, New York, 1952)

A History of London Life, R. J. Mitchell and M. D. R. Leys (Longmans, London, 1958; Longmans, New York, 1958)

The Elizabethans at Home, Elizabeth Barbon & Felix Kelly (Secker & Warburg, London, 1963)

Pharmacy in History, G. E. Trease (Baillière, Tindall & Cox, London, 1964; Williams & Williams, Baltimore, 1965)

A History of the Cost of Living, John Burnett (Penguin, London, 1969)

Shakespeare's England, Levi Fox (Wayland, London, 1972; Putnam, New York, 1972)

The Reformation of the Sixteenth Century, L. W. Cowie (Wayland, London, 1970; Putnam, New York 1970)

Tudor Food and Pastimes, F. G. Emmison (Benn, London, 1964)

The Making of the English Landscape, W. G. Hoskins (Hodder & Stoughton, London, 1955; Penguin, Baltimore, 1970)

ACKNOWLEDGEMENTS

The Publishers wish to express their grateful thanks to all those who have kindly contributed copyright illustrations to this volume: Trustees of the Fitzwilliam Museum, jacket; Trustees of the National Portrait Gallery, frontispiece, 6, 81 (top), 82 (top); Trustees of the British Museum, 7 (bottom), 10, 11, 13 (left), 15 (left), 15 (right bottom), 16 (bottom), 17, 18, 21 (top), 32 (bottom), 33 (top), 34 (top), 36 (bottom), 37 (bottom), 39 (bottom), 41 (top left), 41 (bottom), 46 (top), 65 (left), 68 (bottom), 112; J. R. Freeman Ltd., 8, 9, 13 (right), 15 (right), 19, 22 (bottom), 26 (bottom), 30 (top), 31 (top), 32 (top), 38 (top left), 47 (top left), 49 (top left), 49 (top centre), 49 (bottom left), 66 (right), 72 (top), 76 (bottom), 77 (top right), 81 (bottom), 106 (top), 107 (top), 109, 110 (left), 114–115, 118; Trustees of the London Museum, 16 (top), 38 (top right), 40 (bottom), 41 (top right), 54 (top), 66 (top), 66 (bottom left), 67 (centre), 67 (top right), 70–71, 72 (bottom), 78 (centre right), 80; Radio Times-Hulton Picture Library 20, 27, (bottom), 51 (top left), 56, 68 (top), 69 (top), 73 (top), 75, 77 (top left), 77 (bottom), 82 (bottom), 92, 93, 95, 96, 100, 119, 120 (bottom), 121; Trustees of the Victoria and Albert Museum, 44 (top left), 67 (bottom left), 79, 99 (centre left), 120 (centre); British Tourist Authority, 52; Mansell Collection, 55, 78 (top), 84, 85, 86, 87, 88 (left), 89, 90, 91. The Publishers also gratefully acknowledge the kind permission of the following to reproduce copyright colour pictures on the pages mentioned; British Tourist Authority, 50; British Tourist Authority and Shakespeare Birthplace Trust, 61 (bottom); British Tourist Authority and National Trust, 57; Trustees of the Tate Gallery, 58 (top); Trustees of the British Museum, 58 (bottom); Trustees of the Fitzwilliam Museum, 60–61 (top); National Maritime Museum, Greenwich, 62–63, 64. Other illustrations appearing in this book belong to the Wayland Picture Library.

Index